FLAVORS
of
PANAMA

Nilsa Lasso-von Lang and Jiwanda Gale-Rogers

PublishAmerica
Baltimore

First printing

PublishAmerica has allowed this work to remain exactly as the author intended, verbatim, without editorial input.

Hardcover 9781630041755
Softcover 9781456079819
PUBLISHED BY PUBLISHAMERICA, LLLP
www.publishamerica.com
Baltimore

Printed in the United States of America

I dedicate this book to my closest relatives, especially my mother who helped me collect some of the most traditional family recipes; and my loving husband Karl who is my number-one supporter and traveling partner in life.

Nilsa Lasso-von Lang

I dedicate this book to family and friends, especially my mother Eleanor and my late grandmothers who left their legacy. I also would like to thank my husband Donnie for his support and love during this long journey.

Jiwanda V. Gale-Rogers

Contents

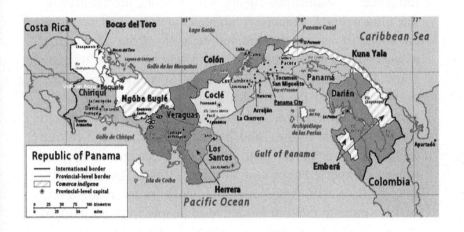

INTRODUCTION

What is Panamanian cuisine? Panamanian cuisine is a unique assortment of different foods from a wide variety of cultures. In her article "Panama Food and Drink," travel writer and author Kirsten Hubbard says: "Because of Panama's diverse Spanish, American, Afro-Caribbean, and indigenous influences, Panamanian cuisine ranges from the familiar to the ultra-exotic." Panama's strategic location has been the backbone of its service-oriented economy from as far back as the colonial period, when this area was famous for its trade paths. The construction of the Panama Canal and its monetary system based on the U.S. dollar since the beginning of the twentieth century have led Panama to become a vital vein for international trading and banking. Currently, a 5-billion dollar project is underway to broaden the Panama Canal. The project is expected to be completed by 2014. Without a doubt, the country's privileged geographic position has made it and will continue to make it attractive to people from all parts of the world. To the Panamanian people, their small country is *Puente del Mundo, Corazón del Universo* (the Bridge of the World and Heart of the Universe), a popular national motto.

Today, Panama is one of the most "ethnically diverse" countries in Central America. This has enriched the Panamanian culture as the people have adopted many of the traditions, holidays, special celebrations, and foods that the newcomers have brought with them. *Flavors of Panama* is the first cookbook about Panamanian cuisine that fuses foods, culture, folklore, history, and tradition. We traveled extensively in Panama and spent a lot of time completing the research and testing for this book. While traveling, we did numerous interviews and searched out the ethnic flavors of Panama. The recipes gathered in this cookbook are provided by our Panamanian relatives, friends, professional chefs, and home cooks. The majority of the recipes were originally written in Spanish. Now, we make this wonderful array of recipes accessible to the English speakers of the world.

Flavors of Panama presents a chronological overview of Panamanian cuisine, drawing attention to indigenous cultures and to the different cultures that have had and continue to have an impact on Panama's gastronomy. It brings together delicious and popular native foods and variations of many cultures, including European and American cuisines, Panamanian-Asian dishes, Afro-Caribbean/ Afro-Hispanic[1] foods, Mexican, South and Central American foods, Indian and Middle Eastern cuisines. It also highlights regional foods and eating patterns. Essentially, the cookbook is divided into 17 recipe sections that include a brief introduction, cooking tips, cultural notes, and a considerable number of gastronomic delights.

Flavors of Panama is a voyage throughout the different regions of Panama, allowing us to appreciate an assortment of typical recipes and diverse cooking styles. We describe the special ingredients that lend regional dishes their characteristic and defining flavor, making clear that, from one region to the next, the same recipes may differ in preparation, ingredients, and cooking tools. At the end, we provide a glossary, a list of Panamanian holidays and celebrations, samples of typical menus, and practical tips for travelers.

1 Afro-Hispanics or Afro-Colonials were black African slaves brought by the Spanish. Afro-Antilleans or Afro-Caribbean slaves were blacks from the Caribbean and West Indies who came to work on the construction of the railroad and then the canal, initially under the French and then completed by the U.S.

PANAMANIAN CUISINE:
HISTORY AND CULTURES

Indigenous Panamanian Foods

Panama's three provincial-level territories or *comarcas* consist of *Kuna Yala* or *San Blas*, *Ngöbe- Buglé* and *Emberá-Wounaan*; and the two sub-provincial indigenous territories are *Kuna de Madugandí* and *Kuna de Wargandí*.[2] The *Kuna* people are the second largest indigenous Amerindian group in Panama. Their ancestors came from Central America to what is now Panama as part of the migratory movement of the *Chibcha* culture to the east of modern Colombia. Today, *Kuna* or *Cuna* people can be found in the San Blas Islands, a group of over 300 islands which are located just off the Caribbean coast of Panama. The indigenous *Kuna Yala* people created what they called "The Republic of Tule" and have self-governing authority over the islands and a part of the mainland. *Kuna de Madugandí* was established in 1996 and it's located in the east part of the province of Panama, in the district of Chepo. *Kuna de Wargandí* is located in the province of Darien. The *Kunas* in the province of Darien are mostly established inland in the deep jungle. *Kuna* people are very friendly. The new generation appears to be losing its culture and traditions through assimilation. Nonetheless, visitors can still experience thousands of years of *Kuna* traditions: dances, music, language, and food. The *Kuna* diet is healthy and basic. Most of their meals usually include fresh seafood, coconut,

2 Seven groups of indigenous people live within the Republic of Panama: Bribri (Costa Rica/Panama), Buglé, Emberá, Kuna, Ngöbe, Teribe (in Bocas del Toro) and Wounaan.

boiled vegetables, and roots. One of their main dishes is *Tule Masi* (a stew-like dish: boiled fish with plantain and coconut). The exposure to western-style foods was limited in the past. In recent times, their cooks have been recognized for their culinary abilities. They have managed to combine their traditional cooking with their acquired knowledge of western cuisine.

The *Emberá-Wounaan* tribes inhabit the province of Darien, the largest and the most heavily forested province of Panama. The two tribes used to be known as *Chocoes* because they emigrated from the Choco province of Colombia to Darien. Linguistically, they are separated. Of the two, *Wounaan* tribe appears to be the least known and the most marginalized indigenous group. Some call the *Emberá-Wounaan* "the river people" because they prefer to live near the rivers. Before the Panamanian government declared part of the rainforest a "national park," their sustainable activities were hunting, fishing, and farming. Traditionally, their main sources of protein came from hunting wild animals. A significant part of their diet came from jungle plants, fruits, heart of palms, and roots. They also eat a lot of seafood. Even though turtles are protected by state regulations and environmentalists, they eat them. *Emberá* delicacies are of two river fish called *Guacuco* and *Sabaleta*. Recent government regulations had forced them to turn to tourism to survive, especially the *Emberá* communities. They are well-known for their incredible handicrafts and for their impressive botanical knowledge. They enjoy painting their bodies with *Jagua*, a natural type of fruit dye. They also use woodcarving for everyday life, such as making canoes, weapons, paddles, furniture, and so on; and carve *Tagua* (a type of nut). Usually, they paint beautiful images of nature and animals on the carved *Tagua* nuts and sell them in the market. They are famous for using natural extracts taken from the earth and plants to create vibrant colors, which are then used to dye their bodies or baskets. For example: annatto is used for red paint and seed pod for orange coloring. Even though some of them have been exposed to the cities and others have been forced to live in modern villages, they seem to prefer their traditional lifestyle in the jungle. In fact, those who have remained in the rainforest still live and dress the way they used to when Europeans arrived. Today, they try to preserve their ancient lifestyles and traditions. They have small gardens near their homes and grow rice, beans, green peas, yuca, *ñame,* and *otoe.* They plant fruit trees, such as lime, orange, cacao, abaca, breadfruit, avocado, and mango. They still manage to grow corn which has been basic to their diet for hundreds of years. The *Emberá* people have gatherings similar to pow-wows, and traditional dances and celebrations where corn is the essential ingredient. For instance, they serve fermented corn drink during a ritual with a *Jaibaná* (medicine man/witch doctor) and members of the community.

The *Ngöbe-Buglé* is an indigenous territory located in the western Panamanian provinces of Bocas del Toro, Chiriqui, Cocle, and Veraguas. They are the largest indigenous group in Panama and have a high degree of administrative autonomy. The *Ngöbe-Buglé* tribes are closely associated and collectively referred to as the *Guaymí* people; however, the *Ngöbe* and *Buglé* are two separate groups of people. Like the other Panamanian tribes, *Ngöbe-Buglé* people use little or no salt in their food. Traditionally, the base of their economy has been agriculture, supplemented by other activities, such as river fishing and hunting. In some cases, they have combined their main sustainable activity (agriculture) with those of the immigrants by raising cattle, chicken, and pigs. Corn and *pixbae* (peach palm fruit) have been central to their diet since the beginning. Popular corn-based foods and drinks are *chicha fuerte* (their favorite fermented corn drink) and *bollo agrio y dulce* (sweet and sour-tasting corn dough). They also grow other crops brought to them by settlers, like rice and beans. *Ngöbe-Buglé* people eat other foods, such as banana balls, plants like *giraca batú* and roots like yuca and *otoe*. They are known for their rudimentary techniques. For example, they still grind corn with stones, and make and use their own bows and spears for hunting.

In summation, the diet of the Panamanian tribes is very similar. Their most typical and traditional foods consist of fresh seafood, roots, *pixbae,* coconut, wild animals, wild birds and, of course, maize which is considered one of the world's largest food crops. The most common crops grown in the indigenous territories, especially in the *Ngöbe -Buglé*, are corn and roots. However, some indigenous groups also grow other grains, fruits and vegetables brought to Panama by immigrants from different parts of the world. They also cultivate plantains, bananas, sugar cane, rice, beans, tomatoes, peppers, and other vegetables in smaller gardens at home. Fruits, such as mango, pineapple, pumpkin, and orange grow seasonally along with cacao. These fruits definitely supplement their diet. A native fruit that has been consumed by Panamanian indigenous people is *nance*, a small tropical fruit that has culinary and beverage uses across Latin America. Meat is rarely eaten although many families keep cows, pigs, ducks, chickens, and still hunt wild animals. Sadly, slash and burn techniques are still in use and soil depletion and deforestation are problems in the indigenous territories.

American and European influences in Panamanian cooking

From as far back as the colonial period, Panama's role as a crossroads for trade has made it a point of interest for Europeans and Americans. They transformed Panamanian cuisine, imposing a meat diet and a "canned and preserved food" type of culture. Wheat flour, one of the pillars in the basic diet of European and North American cultures, was brought to Panama by Europeans and Americans. Oviero and Prado, in their book chapter "Panama: Foods from Other Origins" in *Nuestras Comidas,* list the following European and American foods and ingredients: wheat, barley, oat, rye, bread, wine, oil, lard (of pork), chicken, turkey, duck, goat, hare, pork, meat (cattle farm) and various salads, pastas, cheeses and nuts, vegetables and fruits (cauliflower, lettuce, beets, celery, cabbage, leek, melons, currant and blackberry). They are some of the most important foods in the European and American diets and were passed on to Panamanian culture (117). In Panama, wheat flour-based dishes, and Panamanian meat-based dishes are the result of that European/American impact. The strongly built European and U.S. presence in Panama is justified by the construction of Spanish cities, during the colonial period; the construction of the Panama Railway (1850-1855); and the construction of the Panama Canal. First, the disastrous French Canal project (1882-1902), and subsequently the successful completion of the Canal project by the U.S. government (1904-1914). Oviero and Prado state that the American culture was evident with the establishment of military bases in the Canal Zone, American supermarkets and American products: "canned and preserved foods, sodas, borboun wisky, kool-aid, hot dogs, turkey, pancakes with syrup, peanut butter, nuts, corn flakes, Southern-style roast pork and eggs with bacon, and junk food. Consequently, eating turkey, roast pork, apples, grapes, peaches and pears for Christmas celebrations soon became popular in Panama" (119). Nowadays, there are several American-style supermarkets throughout the country. Fast food restaurants are in every major city.

Today, many travelers, investors, retirees, and expats are relocating to Panama City, and to the highlands and coastal regions. According to Panamanian builders and contractors, about 90% of retirees relocating to Panama are Americans and the remaining 10% are Canadians and Europeans. Panama is rated as one of the best places in the Americas for retirement by the *International Living Magazine*. This is based on its modern infrastructure, investment opportunities, business-friendly government, safety, climate, beauty, attractions, cost of living, pensioner's residency programs, well-developed domestic and international facilities, well-developed services sector, high quality health care, and much more. *Forbes* ranks Panama as "#60 Best Country for Business." *New York Times* reports: "At the crossroads of two oceans and two continents, Panama City is a dynamic metropolis. That's never been truer than it is today. Everywhere in this steamy, tropical town are foreign investors talking shop in upscale cafes, expat fortune-seekers toasting their fates in wine bars, cranes stalking the rooftops of a skyline that seems to grow before your eyes." Panama is awakening to its potential and it is attracting many foreigners, especially Americans and Canadians. It is evident that American and European cultures and foods continue to impact Panamanian gastronomy and the other way around.

Afro-Caribbean/Afro-Hispanic Foods

According to Panamanian history, the first black slaves who arrived to Panama were brought by Europeans from Guinea, Senegal, and Angola. They were known as Afro-Hispanics or Afro-Colonials. This group was vital in the colonial system because slaves were used mainly to transport merchandise that went through *Camino Real* o *Camino de Cruces* (important colonial trade paths). They also were utilized as construction workers to build the Cities of *Nombre de Dios* and Colonial Panama. Some slaves escaped and became thieves or guides for pirates. Another group was the Afro-Antillean/Afro-Caribbean slaves, mainly from the West Indies. They were brought in the nineteenth century to work on the construction of the railway. In 1851, slavery was abolished in the Republic of New Granada (present-day country of Colombia: Panama was Colombian territory until 1903). Many Afro-Caribbean workers were free to return to their native land. In the early twentieth century, they came back and stayed to work as laborers on the construction of the Panama Canal. Today, Afro-Panamanians represent a large segment of the population in the provinces of Panama, Colon, Darien and Bocas del Toro. Most recently, Panamanians have learned to embrace their African heritage through celebrations, such as *Día de la Etnia* (African Heritage Day), in the month of May. They celebrate with traditional dances, songs, and various Afro-Panamanian dishes. African culture is well-built in these parts of the country; therefore, their tremendous contribution to Panamanian food is undeniable. Oviero and Prado confirm that African people brought in "palm oil, *ñame*, date, olive, fig, ackee, coffee, callaloo, Arabian onion, melons, tamarind, and various spices" (118). The Afro-Caribbean immigrants introduced to Panama a variety of dishes and ingredients. The Afro-Caribbean food fairs/festivals are very well-liked among Panamanians. The most popular dishes are "Bar-B-Q chicken, *gallo pinto* or spotted rooster, dry codfish and potato, *bacalao* balls, *fufu* (seafood soup), dumplings, *cu cu* (corn cream with tender okra), *patí* (puff pastry or empanada stuffed with spicy beef), saus or pickled pork feet, and beef stew" (118). In addition, there are Barbadian blend of spices _ thyme, marjoram, green onions, parsley to name a few.

Other important contribution is *bon* or *bun* (sweet bread), a Caribbean bread-style served during Holy Week. Most of the dishes listed above are also very popular in food stands set up during the annual Black Christ or Christ of Nazareth celebrations and the dance *El Tambor de los Congos* (The Congos' Drums) performed during Carnival in the province of Colon. The dance is a mockery of the Spanish Kings; it is a mix of the Catholic practices and Afro-Antillean traditions, dating back from slavery.

Panamanian-Chinese Cuisine

In Panama one can observe a strong cultural influence from Asia. The Chinese culture is unmistakably the most prominent of all. Mon, in his article "Chinese Immigrants in Panama," reports that most of the Chinese who came to Panama were from southern China. The first wave of immigrants was motivated by the California Gold Rush (1848) and the construction of the Transcontinental Railway (1850-1855). Since Panama appeared to be the easiest and safest way to get to the west coast of the U.S., this route became a point of interest for people from all over the world. The Railroad Company had initially hired black descendants of old slaves to do the heavy work but, later on, the need for more laborers compelled them to hire people from any ethnic groups. Waves of Chinese people came to work on the construction of the Panama Canal. After the black population of Antilleans, the Chinese were the largest group of immigrants in Panama. Although the Chinese people were hired to work as laborers on both monumental projects (Railroad and Canal), they transitioned over generations from laborers to merchants/small business owners. The majority of them walked away from their heavy duties. Before long, most Chinese established kiosks, small stores, mini-markets, supermarkets, motels, restaurants and bought small pieces of property (53-60, 71). The Asian contribution to Panamanian food has been, without a doubt, very remarkable. Oviero and Prado list the following foods and ingredients: rice, coffee, cinnamon, whole cloves, garlic, onion, Chinese parsley or coriander, small onion, quince, basil, oregano, mustard, lentils, soy bean, banana, plantain, ginger, among others" (117-118). Today, all these products are essential to the Panamanian diet. In the last few years, numerous Asian restaurants have opened their doors (Cantonese, Japanese, Thai, and Korean), especially across Panama City. *Travelchannel.com* reported that Panama has the oldest China Town in the Americas and it's located almost on the heart of the capital. Chinese restaurants can also be found across the country. According to Professor Diana Chan, Chinese people celebrate traditional festivities based on the Chinese Calendar. Panamanian-Chinese observe the holidays on January 1 and 2. On the first day, they eat traditional light foods: *Lo Hon Chai, Chin Toi* and others. The major celebrations take place on the second day (5).

Indian and Middle Eastern Cuisines in Panama

In addition to all the previously mentioned cultural groups that have impacted Panama's gastronomy, there are others, such as Jews, Hindus, and Arabs. De Castro, in his article "Jews in Panama," indicates that Jews came to Panama during the California Gold Rush and the construction of the Transcontinental Railway. The first groups of Jewish immigrants were the Sephardic Jews who came from Curaçao, Jamaica, and Saint Thomas where they had settled, after leaving Spain and the Mediterranean region. There are reasons to believe that other Jews came with the Spanish during colonial times and later on they were assimilated into the culture (96-97). Other groups of immigrant Jews (Sephardic and Ashkenazi) came during the construction of the Panama Canal. Other waves included Jews who came after WWI and WWII, escaping from the Nazi persecution. The last wave of Jews came from the Middle East. The Jewish community in Panama has kept its traditional practices, including the consumption of *Kosher* foods, available at all *Kosher* supermarkets, bakeries, and restaurants. Non-Jewish Panamanians also shop at these establishments because of the freshness of their foods: meats, dairy products, breads, and other baked goods. It is noteworthy to mention that the *Rosca Navideña*, very popular among Panamanians during Christmas, is what the Jews called *Challah* bread which is an important part of their tradition.

Another significant number of immigrants came from India. According to Perez, Gandhi, and Shahani's study, Hindu people came to work as laborers on the two monumental construction projects in the Isthmus: the Railway and the Canal. After the Panama Canal was completed, the majority stayed in the cities of Panama and Colon. Some of them settled down as small business owners. At first, like many other immigrants, they suffered discrimination but eventually they gained a place in Panamanian society (107, 126). Their rich culture has certainly added new flavors to Panamanian cooking. For instance, they brought with them various spices, like the curries; and vegetables, like eggplant. They get credit for the numerous Indian dishes Panamanians enjoy today, such as "*samosas, Juab Jamul* and *Rusgula*" (135). The Arab culture has also impacted Panamanian cuisine. In Panama, it's a known fact that *arroz con leche* (rice pudding) is one of the major Middle Eastern culinary contributions to our cuisine.

Latin American Impact in Panamanian Gastronomy

Panama's cuisine has also been influenced by its neighbors: Central and South America, Mexico, and the Caribbean countries. Consequently, some Panamanian dishes bear similarities with those of other Latin American nations. For instance, different styles of corn *tortillas* are made throughout Latin America. Panama, Costa Rica and Nicaragua share dishes like *gallo pinto* (spotted rooster); Panama and Mexico serve a sorrel drink _ known as *saril (hibiscus*) in Panama and *agua de jamaica* in Mexico; Panama and Puerto Rico serve fried plantains _ known as *patacones* in Panama and *tostones* in Puerto Rico; Ecuador and Panama serve *carne en palito(s) (*skewer beef). In Latin America, there are a number of regional varieties of *chichas* (drinks*)* which are prepared and served in most South and Central American countries, including Panama. Particularly, *chicha* of maize has been consumed by indigenous people of Latin America for many years. Most of these indigenous cultures use *chicha* of maize for ritual purposes and consume it in vast quantities during community parties and religious celebrations. One can find similarities between Panamanian and many Columbian foods, for example *patacones* and *sancocho*. This is not surprising, since Panama was a province of Colombia before 1903 and it inherited some Colombian dishes and ingredients. Some ingredients from Central and South America and Mexico are also part of the Panamanian diet (see glossary). The impact the rest of Latin American countries has had on Panama's cuisine is evident. However, each country gives its dishes a very unique regional flavor.

REGIONAL FOODS AND EATING PATTERNS

Gastronomy of Panama City, Colon and Environs

It's no surprise that the biggest variety of dishes is found in Panama City and the surrounding areas: from the capital, Panama City, through the historic Casco Viejo or French Quarter, Old Panama, China town, the Panama Canal area; northeast into the towns of Chepo and Bayano; northwest into the province of Colon; and southwest into the city of La Chorrera. Panama is a melting pot of ethnicities, and its cuisine is accordingly influenced by its diverse population. One can find excellent food in restaurants from all over the world: five-star French, Italian, Middle Eastern, Indian, Chinese, Japanese, Greek, and others.

Urban families eat three meals a day: breakfast, lunch, and dinner. Breakfast and dinner are usually hearty meals; lunch is typically light. Just like in the U.S., eating times and dining patterns vary a lot among urban dwellers. **A typical breakfast** is a selection of fried meats, fresh rolls or bread, *hojaldras/ hojaldres* or *arepas* (fried bread), deep-fried corn tortillas with white cheese, scrambled eggs, fritters, and sautéed liver. Coffee is the most common breakfast drink. The desserts and juices for breakfast are usually made of a tropical fruit in season. **A typical lunch** may begin with soup, followed by small portions of chicken, steak or seafood, or a stew with white rice, or a small portion of any of the following: rice with coconut, rice with green pigeon peas and coconut, rice with beans, rice with seafood. Lunch may include a small bowl of beans or lentils and a small salad or slices of the fruit in season. A bowl *of sancocho*, a traditional chicken soup, is a typical lunch. For Panamanians lunch is not considered the main meal. This is why the portions are usually small. **A typical dinner** is similar to a typical lunch but the portions are much larger. Dinner may consist of meat, poultry, seafood, rice (any of the styles listed above), beans, fruit, and salad. Beef and/or seafood stews are very common in Panama. Traditional recipes are corn tamales, Panamanian-style rice with chicken and chicken *sanchocho* (soup). Wrapped corn tamales are considered the main national dish. Corn tamales and Panamanian-style rice with chicken are made for special occasions. Quite a few Panamanian foods are fried, especially at local *fondas* (food stands) or fritter stands. Some of the most popular are twice-fried plantains, plantain chips, fried yuca, stuffed yuca, empanadas, corn tortillas, fried bread, just to mention a few. Most of the fried dishes listed above are considered appetizers or little bites. Like in most of the country, seafood is excellent and in abundant throughout the provinces of Panama and Colon. Panama's favorite seafood appetizer is *Ceviche* (made with raw seafood, lemon and/or lime juice, and some spices). Fish is also central to Panamanian diet, especially around Holy Week. On Good Friday is customary to eat fresh fish. The majority of Panamanians are Roman Catholics. Their tradition dictates that no one should eat red meat on Good Friday. As a result, most Panamanian Catholics do not serve any red meat on Good Friday. This is especially true in the rural regions where people are more traditional (see sample menus on pages 501-507).

In the northeast of Panama, one finds the towns of Chepo and Bayano. Chepo is a small town that is nearly a suburb of Panama City. The Afro-Panamanian culture and diet are embedded in this region. The town of Bayano or El llano also has a very strong African influence. It was named after a legendary African slave who led the most famous of the slave revolts of sixteenth century Panama. Bayano almost mimics Chepo's daily diet. Although there is a stronger indigenous influence in the diet of this region due to the existence of a Kuna reservation called *Bayano Kuna* located in the upper Rio Bayano area.

The province of Colon is located northwest of Panama City, facing the Atlantic. The Spanish first set foot on this region in 1501. Colon's position made it a famous trading post back in the sixteenth and seventeenth century and has become so again in modern times, hosting the largest port system in Latin America. It is the most important Free Trade Zone in the east and is the second biggest center of imports and redistribution in the world. The city of Colon is the Atlantic port of entrance and exit for the Panama Canal. This province is divided into five districts: Colon, the second largest city after Panama City; Chagres, the smallest district; Donoso, located west of Chagres; Santa Isabel and its important capital Palenque, located east of Portobelo; and the district of Portobelo, named by Christopher Columbus *Porto Bello*, which means beautiful bay. The town of Portobelo is famous among tourists because of its ruins. The ruins of Spanish fortresses and cannons confirm the vitality of Portobelo during colonial times. In 1980, this historic area was declared a world heritage site by the UNESCO. Portobelo City is also known for the Black Christ Festival on October 21. This is a Portobelo fair to honor the locals' patron saint *Cristo Negro* or *Black Christ*. Every year, thousands of devotees from all over the world make the pilgrimage.

It is evident that Colon's cooking has been influenced by Spanish Colonial, Afro- Hispanic, Afro-Caribbean, European/ American, and Asian cultures. Historically and culturally, Panama has had two distinct groups of blacks: The Afro-Colonials and the Afro-Antilleans. An important fact is that Colon was the port of entry for thousands of Antilleans, especially blacks from Jamaica and Barbados who came to work on the construction of the Railway and then the Canal. Currently, the Afro-Panamanians represent the majority of Colon's population.

Colon's cuisine is definitely very diverse. Some of the foods and dishes served daily and during the local festivities are dishes based on seafood, chicken, pork, and beef. Fish, which can be found in a great diversity, is usually fried, steamed or roasted. Octopus in coconut sauce is also a popular dish. There are other varieties of seafood dishes: King crab, crab, shrimp, *cambombia* (Conch), and snail. Some locals still eat turtle soup and turtle eggs, in spite of recent government regulations and environmentalists' efforts to save eggs and turtles from human consumption. Poultry is used to prepare dishes similar to those of traditional Afro- Hispanic and Afro-Caribbean cuisines. People from Colon smoke ham and also jerk pork or chicken which are known to be of Jamaican origin. Chicken-based dishes are numerous and feature a variety of vegetables, fruits, and Afro-Caribbean cooking herbs and spices. Pork is also very popular in this region. A very common dish is *gallo pinto* (spotted rooster) which is made of rice, beans, and pork.

As mentioned previously, *bon* or *bun* is an important Afro-Caribbean contribution to Panamanian cuisine and religious believes. In her article entitled "Bon, la tradición del pan para la Semana Santa en Colón," Migdalia Grinard stresses the importance of the *bon* in Colon during Holy Week: "it is known as sweet bread with fruit and raisins and it is on the table of all households in Colon around these dates because it is a religious tradition… it means the time of peace and love has arrived." She adds: "A cross made with pieces of the same dough is placed on the center of the bread, representing the cross where Jesus was crucified." The older population of Colon affirms that *bon* had a religious meaning for Antilleans who came to Panama to work on the Canal and they brought this tradition to Panama.

Like other provinces, Colon celebrates its history and people by combining food, folklore, and culture at traditional festivities, such as *Diablos* and *Congo* Festival, Black Christ of Portobelo Festival, and Cocle del Norte Festival. As indicated above, the dishes served during especial events are based on seafood, chicken, pork, and beef. There are, however, other agricultural products like corn, rice, and *barojo* to make *barojo* jelly. This delicious jelly is sold at the Cocle del Norte Festival. Jaén Espinosa points out that this festival "…honors the multicultural heritage of the region… population is represented by Afro-Panamanians, indigenous people, and immigrants from Azuero Peninsula." In addition to traditional dishes and handicrafts, the Cocle del Norte Festival offers the opportunity to enjoy *congo* dances and the traditional dance of the *Cucua* Devils.

Traditional Countryside Cuisine

The central provinces of Panama: Cocle, Herrera, Los Santos, and Veraguas, are the home of a large part of what Panamanians consider their folklore with typical homemade meals, Carnivals, and religious celebrations. In these provinces, traditional Panamanian cuisine is an overlapping mix of various cultures, especially the indigenous and European cuisines. This region incorporates a variety of grains, tropical fruits, vegetables, roots, and herbs. Cocle is primarily an agricultural area, with sugar and tomatoes as major crops. Penonome, the capital of Cocle, plays a very important role in Panama's agricultural industry. Throughout the capital one can find various typical Spanish Colonial and indigenous recipes that have suffered very few changes. Penonome is also a very festive town and prides itself on the Aquatic Carnivals, the Orange Festival, Tomato Festival, and the Sugar Cane Festival. Another outstanding city of Cocle is Aguadulce which literally means "sweet water" in Spanish. It has been known for years as the land of salt and sugar.

The provinces of Herrera and Los Santos make up what is called the *Azuero* Peninsula. The province of Veraguas extends into it on the west side of this peninsula. It is a known fact that the *Azuero* region was one of the first parts of Panama to be settled and cultivated thousands of years before the arrival of the Spaniards. Today, much of the land has been cleared for cultivation or grazing. Eating patterns are very similar throughout these regions. Rural families eat only two meals a day. In fact, some people skip lunch all together because they are accustomed to eating a hearty breakfast and a large dinner in late afternoon or early evening.

During Holy Week, people from the *Azuero* Peninsula prepare and sell traditional homemade sweets, such as mango jelly, *cabanga*, cashew fruit marmalade or jelly, cocada with cashew, among others.

The provinces of Bocas del Toro and Chiriqui structure the Western Mountains and Coastal Regions. The province of Chiriqui is located in the western coast of Panama. This province has the tallest mountains, longest rivers, most fertile valleys, spectacular highland rainforest, and a rich diversity of marine life. It is also the nation's most productive agricultural and cattle-ranching region. Panamanian famers as well as European and American settlers have viewed the climate and slopes of the Chiriqui highlands as prime for coffee, timber, and other crops. Their descendants still work the fields today. Bocas del Toro is situated north of Chiriqui and it consists of nine islands, 52 keys and some 200 tiny islets. Interestingly, the Bocas del Toro Archipielago is named after a rock that resembles a bull (Toro in Spanish) and it is located in the Island of Bastimento. It doesn't offer cool temperatures or high-altitude thrills like Chiriqui, but it has its own distinct Caribbean attraction, like pristine beaches and an amazing variety of marine life. Bocas del Toro is among the banana exporters since the late nineteenth century. The gastronomy of Bocas del Toro and Chiriqui embraces traditional cuisine, as well as a selection of dishes from diverse cultures. One can especially appreciate the indigenous, Spanish, Afro-Caribbean, and American cultures and foods.

A **typical country breakfast** may include coffee, milk, fruit juice, pork rinds, corn tortillas, scrambled eggs, national fresh white pressed cheese, corn *bollo* (corn meal dough boiled in its corn husks, plantain leaves or Royal Palm tree leaves), fresh local breads, fruit in season, *cuchifrito* (organ meats), beef and/or liver and onions, pork, national chorizos, yellow split pea fritters, yuca root, or *hojaldres*. **A typical country lunch and dinner** will include *carimañolas* (stuffed yucca), fried and boiled yuca root, white rice, beans, lentils, corn and flour *empanadas*, corn tortilla, corn fritters, pork rinds, cow tongue, chicken stew, *sancocho* or country-style chicken soup, potato or vegetable salads, dry-salted beef stew, *tasajo* (smoked and cured beef), rice with chicken, rice with green pigeon peas and coconut, pork, beef, fresh corn *bollos, serén* or corn soup, fried plantains, tamale casserole, corn balls with cheese, *zambo serén,* shredded beef, *zurrapa, guacho, ceviche, mondongo or* Panamanian-style tripe stew*, conserva, alfajor*, various fruits, iguana, and other wild animals. Many Panamanians drink coffee after dinner; in fact, they might drink several cups of coffee a day. Like in the rest of the country, plantains and yuca, along with white rice or coconut rice and beans are the standard accompaniment to traditional dishes. Some dishes are eaten on and off and for holidays, special celebrations, and national or local fairs throughout Panama. For example, tamales, rice with chicken, soups, roast pork, skewer beef or beef on the stick, fritters, various fried roots, and Panamanian-style potato salad (see sample menus on pages 501-507).

Evidently, the gastronomy within this area of the country is very alike. However, each province has few unique dishes. For instance, yuca root *al mojo, guisado de papaya* or stew papaya, and *mangungo* corn soup are unique to the province of Herrera. Rincón Tableño chicken, green plantain tortilla, *fututiado* rice, pumpkin salad and stuffed pork are, because of the way they are made, exclusive to Los Santos. In the province of Veraguas, it is very common to serve fresh water shrimp soup and rice with *chiro* (small fresh water shrimp). For Holy Week, it is customary to eat fresh water grilled sardine. A stew pumpkin and a fish soup like *salpreso* are believed to be from Veraguas. A homemade sausage, like *morcilla de gallina* is one of Veraguas's favorites. Pigeon broth and sour milk (with salt or sugar) are considered remedies for the sick. *Conserva* (boiled cane syrup with cashew nut seeds), orange flan, and sour orange candy are thought to be from Veraguas. *The Guacho en Totuma* Festival is an annual celebration in Atalaya, Veraguas (April or May). This festival gives people the opportunity to enjoy and appreciate Panamanian music, dances, handicrafts, and delicious dishes. One of the most important dishes in this festival is the *guacho*. Basically, this is a rice-based dish. The *guacho* is served in *totumas* made of *calabazo* (calabash or gourd). Using *totumas* to serve food and water is a tradition that takes people back in time, since *totumas* were commonly used as kitchen utensils by indigenous people. Today, *totumas* are still used in the countryside, mainly by indigenous people and peasants.

In Chiriqui, *bollo* de cuajá (baked corn dough prepared with milk and a lot of cheese) is only one of its kind. Palmito cheese is one of Chiriqui's favorites. *Bienmesabe chiricano,* a traditional dessert, is prepared with fresh raw milk, rice, panela, and spices. *Chiriqui's sancocho* (chicken soup) is very unique. The chicken *sanchocho* of Chiriqui is heavier or thicker than *sancochos* prepared in any other parts of the country because they add more vegetables, legumes, and roots. In the city of Tole, Chiriqui a very typical dish is *guacho chiricano* (salted beef, yuca, onion, culantro, pepper, and shoot of *otoe* plant). For Christmas they make sweet corn tamales, roasted pork, and *bollos chiricanos* (sweetened corn dough wrapped in plantain leaves). In Holy Week is habitual to serve lima bean soup with panela. For this special holiday, people also prepare traditional homemade sweets and breads, such as rolls, cocadas, cashew nuts, suspiros, and many others. These breads and sweets are sold just outside the homes or they are given to friends and/or relatives. Oviero and Rivera inform that sponge cake soaked in syrup and rum is a popular cake at weddings. It is prepared for this special occasion because people believe that this cake will bring good fortune to the newlyweds. Another dish with special magic powers is chicken with ginger_ people from Chiriqui believe this dish will bring them good luck and serve it on Sundays when the lottery is played. On Sundays, they also prepare spaghetti with chicken and potato salad with beet. An important festival centers on a dish called *Mono en Bijao*. In fact, the festival is named after this dish. Tamara Ponce explains that *The Mono en Bijao* Festival honors the old tradition of the *mono*. Literally, *mono* means monkey; however, in this context, the word *mono* represents the traditional lunch of the peasants from the Chiriqui Province. This dish is essentially rice and beans with *tajadas* (fried ripe plantains) and beef, pork, sausage or chicken wrapped in bijao leaves. The name "monkey" came from a traditional practice. In the past, workers out in the field used to hang it from a tree to keep it away from insects and animals, from then on it was called *mono en bijao*.

Another meaningful countryside celebration is *La Matanza* or the slaughtering of the cow. Jaén Espinosa says: "*La Matanza* is a traditional family gathering in the countryside of Panama." The cow is selected and slaughtered at dawn the day before the actual celebration takes place. Men cut the meat and women cook various dishes, such as grilled meat, corn tortillas, fried tapioca, soups, and stews. The purpose of *La Matanza* is to bring together the community and celebrate birthdays, weddings or any other special event. It can serve as a fundraising event to help members of the community who are in need of medical treatment and do not have the means to pay for it. It can also help raise funds for local carnival festivities. Panamanians have the opportunity to appreciate their own culture through traditional dishes and typical music, for example: *tamborito, pindin,* and *murga.*

Like in Colon, the Afro-Caribbean influence in the cooking of Bocas del Toro is irrefutable. Some of the most common dishes are stuffed fish, cu cu, codfish with ackee, Escovitch or Escoviched fish, saus or pickled pork feet, pumpkin rice, ground food, one pot, roasted chicken, chile with meat, the famous *Rum Down* or *Rondon* (fish, lobster or dry cod with coconut milk), fish head soup with *ñame,* turtle stew, breaded turtle, shark, turtle's flipper soup, rice with crab, rice with fish, beans and salted pigtail soup, isleño fried fish, Journal Cake, rice and beans, *guacho bocatoreño,* callaloo or kallaloo soup with eggs, cow foot soup, lentils, beans, Rondon of sardine or coconut soup, rice with lentils and coconut, rice and beans, rice with ahuyama and pork tail, meat balls, chicken chow mein, spaghetti with chicken, potato and codfish, lobster in sauce, shrimp in coconut sauce, grilled and breaded steak. **Snacks:** bakes or dumplings, codfish cake, patties or patí or patty isleño bocatoreño, plantain tarts or *plantinta,* banana fritters, vegetable rounds. **Afro-Panamanian- style breads:** enyucado o yuca pone, coconut bread, banana nut bread, perfect corn bread, ginger bread, bon or bun, hot cross bun, and zucchini bread.

Afro-Darienita communities and other immigrants have had a tremendous impact in the cooking of the province of Darien. Most historians accept as true that the first Afro-Hispanics in Panama were the black slaves brought to the provinces of

Panama and Colon by the Spanish, during the colonial period. Eventually, some of them moved to other provinces, including Darien. However, there are historians like Peter Martyr who defended the theory that there were Africans in Panama before the arrival of the Europeans. He believes that a group of Africans sailed the sea, probably as "Ethiopian pirates," and disembarked near the coast of Darien. Soon after, they took refuge in this large and heavily forested province *(revistacaoba. com* and *afrohispanos.org*). Historians may disagree about when and how the African people settled in Darien. Even so, one thing is for sure, the African culture has had a strong and direct cultural impact on this region. For instance, locals reassure that *El Bunde*, a popular religious festivity, is also known as the "Authentic Panamanian Christmas" because they sing and dance *bundes* and *loas* or native Christmas songs with lyrics that talk about the arrival of the baby Jesus. It is celebrated from December 6 to January 6 by the *Afro-Darienitas* from the town of Garachiné. The most important ceremony takes place on December 24. Plenty of foods and drinks are served during these celebrations. Some of the most popular Afro-Darienita dishes are *tapao garachineño*, angel hair, stuffed squid, *bollera/bollería* (a plantain-based dish also known as *goyoría).*

Other groups that can be included in this region are the *Hispano-Indígenas,* as naturalist Hernán Araúz calls them. They are famers that came from the countryside to work on the highway of Darien (1970). They live mostly in towns along the highway. They call Darien their home and brought with them the farming and ranching ways of life, which has caused deforestation in the region. As expected, the presence of these immigrants has created social tension.

People in Darien eat a lot of seafood and preserved meats. The residents of La Palma, the capital, are very fond of fish, for example: *piangua* in coconut milk, yellow sea bass, and the *guabina*. They eat fried plantains with meats. One of their favorites is the locally produced *plátano popocho* or plantain with four points. They also consumed salted, smoked or preserved meats because of the lack of refrigeration. For example, pig tails and red kidney beans is a very common dish. The pig tails are imported from Canada in barrels. Franks cooked with onions and tomato sauce or *salchichas guisadas* are other preserved meats served with fried bread at breakfast. Some of them still eat wild animals like wild boar, wild rabbit, and iguana.

Popular Desserts, Juices and Drinks, and Alcoholic Beverages across the Nation:

There is a huge variety of Panamanian desserts and sweets, juices, cold and hot drinks, and a fair selection of alcoholic beverages. Desserts and sweets are made of milk, eggs, coconut, fruit, cane syrup, flour, rice, corn, root vegetables and tubers, legumes, and vegetables. Natural fruit juices, corn, rice, coconut, and plant and flower drinks, commonly known as *chichas*, are always readily available. Shakes come in many different flavors, depending on the fruit in season. Also on hand are coffees and medicinal teas. Some common Panamanian alcoholic drinks are wines, rums, beers, fermented corn drinks, seaweed and cane syrup, and of course, fermented sugar cane, like the Panamanian national liquor, called *Seco Herrerano*.

RECIPES

APPETIZERS
AND
LITTLE BITES

P anama has a good selection of fast and tasty appetizer recipes. The most common appetizers and small bites served at lunch or dinner are *patacones* (twice-fried green plantains), fried yuca, *carimañolas* (stuffed-yuca), corn and flour empanadas, and of course, ceviche, Panama's favorite seafood appetizer. Ceviche is fresh raw fish or seafood marinated in fresh lemon juice and/or lime juice. The citrus cooks the raw fish and shellfish. This is a traditional dish known to be popular in Central and South America. Each country has a unique way of preparing it. For instance, in Panama one can find different styles of ceviche: traditional or Sea Bass ceviche, shrimp, young shark and a combination of seafood. The traditional Panamanian ceviche is made with a fish called corvina or Chilean Sea Bass, a mixture of lemon and/or lime juice and pieces of celery are added; Mexicans add tomatoes and salsa to their ceviche; and Peruvians add sweet corn and potatoes to theirs. *Note: Plantain has its own section due to the numerous plantain recipes. For twice-fried green plantains, plantain chips, plantain empanadas, banana fritters, and other plantain and banana recipes see the section* **PLANTAINS AND BANANAS**.

Traditional Panamanian Ceviche

(Ceviche de corvina)

Serves 4

Ingredients:

1 pound fresh boneless sea bass (corvina)

1½ cups finely chopped onion (white or red)

½ cup finely chopped celery

¼ cup finely chopped fresh culantro (or parsley)

1 cup fresh lemon juice

1 cup fresh lime juice

Salt and pepper to taste

1 seeded and finely minced habanero pepper

Preparation:

Cut fish into bite-size pieces and put it in a glass bowl.

Add all other ingredients, mixing well. The lemon juice should cover fish.

Cover glass bowl with plastic wrap.

Refrigerate at least 24 hours. Allow one day for fish to cook in lemon juice and onions.

Serve in goblets with crackers or saltines on the side.

CULTURAL NOTE: *In Panama, it is popular to serve ceviche in small paper cups.*

TIPS: *Can substitute Sea Bass with any firm FRESH white fish, such as red snapper or swordfish.*

VARIATION: *Combine fresh ½ pound of each of the following: squid, octopus, scallops, clams, lobster, and crab. Cut into small bite-size pieces and mix with ingredients listed on this recipe.*

Improvise by adding ½ cup cubed mango or pineapple.

Fish Ceviche

(Ceviche de pescado)

Serves 8

Ingredients:

2 pounds fresh fish fillets

2 chopped small onions

1 ½ cups lemon juice

1 teaspoon salt

1 seeded and chopped hot chile pepper or habanero pepper

1 tablespoon gin

2 tablespoons olive oil

Preparation:

Cut fish into small bite-size pieces and put it in a glass bowl.

Add all ingredients and mix well. Refrigerate at least 24 hours.

Serve in goblets with crackers on the side.

NOTE: This is a variation of the previous recipe.

Shrimp Ceviche
(Ceviche de camarones)

Serves 8 to 10

Ingredients:

2 pounds fresh peeled and deveined shrimp

½ cup fresh lime juice

1 cup fresh lemon juice

1 chopped large onion

1 seeded and finely chopped red bell pepper

3 seeded and finely chopped habanero peppers

¼ cup finely chopped fresh parsley

¼ cup finely chopped fresh culantro

Preparation:

Cut each shrimp into about 4 or 5 pieces, depending on size.

Squeeze limes/lemons and pour juices into a glass bowl. Put cut-up shrimp, onion, peppers, parsley, and culantro in the bowl.

Mix well and refrigerate at least 24 hours.

Serve with saltine crackers.

TIPS: *Use more limes if they are not juicy. To get more juice from limes put in microwave for 1 minute but peel them to avoid a bitter flavor. If not hot enough, add a few drops of your favorite hot sauce.*

VARIATION: *Young shark ceviche can be made the same way. Use 4 shark fillets, skinned and cut into small bite-size pieces.*

Angels on Horseback

Serves 4

Ingredients:

20 large shucked fresh oysters

10 slices bacon

½ teaspoon salt

Dash black pepper

Dash paprika

3 tablespoons chopped fresh or dry parsley

Preparation:

Drain oysters. Lay an oyster across ½ slice of bacon.

Season oysters and add parsley. Roll strip of bacon around oyster and fasten with toothpicks.

Place oyster on a rack in a shallow baking dish.

Bake, uncovered, in a preheated 450°F oven about 10 minutes, or until bacon is crisp.

Remove toothpicks and serve.

Carimañolas

Serves 16 to 18

Ingredients for dough:

4 pounds peeled and cubed yuca root (2-inch cubes)

1 tablespoon salt

Ingredients for filling:

1 pound lean ground beef

1 tablespoon olive oil or canola oil

½ cup finely chopped onion

2 minced garlic cloves

Salt and black pepper to taste

Pinch ground thyme

1 cup tomato sauce

Preparation for yuca dough:

Boil yuca in a large pot; add salt and cook until tender. Do not overcook yuca.

Filling:

In a medium skillet heat oil; cook and stir onion until translucent.

Add ground beef to onion and cook, breaking up the meat with a wooden spoon until no pink remains.

Add thyme, garlic, and tomato sauce. Simmer over moderate heat and stir frequently for 3 minutes, or until liquid has nearly evaporated.

Season to taste with salt and pepper. Let cool for a few minutes.

Making carimañolas:

Drain yuca and mash with a potato masher. Add more salt, if needed.

Wet hands and roll a portion of about ½ cup of the mixture into a ball. Make a deep indentation in the ball and place a spoonful of the filling in the center of dimple. Work the dough back around the filling, making sure the filling is covered with dough. Stretch ball a little until it looks elongated.

Deep-fry in hot oil two at a time until golden brown. Drain on paper towels.

Serve warm and enjoy the buttery flavor of yuca!

Yellow Split Pea Fritters
(Torrejas de arvejas)

Serves 10 to 12

Ingredients:

1 pound yellow split peas

1 large finely chopped onion

1 teaspoon salt

1 teaspoon sugar

1 teaspoon baking powder

1 beaten egg

Canola oil (for frying)

Preparation:

Soak split peas 8 to 12 hours, or overnight.

Next day, drain all the water and grind.

Add salt, sugar, baking powder, egg, and onion.

Mix well and spoon-mix into hot oil; Deep-fry until golden brown.

Saus

Serves 12 to 14

Ingredients:

4 pounds pork feet

1 tablespoon salt

3 medium onions

¼ cup chopped chives

4 cucumbers

1 ½ cups lime juice

2 hot peppers

2 cups water

¼ cup canola oil

Preparation:

Clean pig's feet with a brush and put in a pan to cook with enough water, until they are soft. Let them cool and then rinse them with cold water.

Put pig's feet in a glass bowl. Cut onions into small pieces and put them on top.

Mix lime juice, salt, oil, and water.

Cut hot peppers into small pieces and discard seeds.

Peel and cut cucumbers into thin slices and place them over onions.

Pour liquid mix and stir with a wooden spoon.

Cover the bowl with plastic wrap and leave in the refrigerator overnight.

Garnish with chopped chives on top.

CULTURAL NOTE: This pickled pig's feet recipe was brought to Panama by Afro-Antillean immigrant workers, during the construction of the Panama Canal. Saus, as it is known in Panama, is really considered an appetizer. It is served as a cold dish at parties, meetings, national celebrations, and even at weddings. It is very popular and famous for its spicy and vinegary flavors. This dish is very often served in small portions at food stands during local and national fairs, and other special holidays and celebrations, such as weddings, birthdays, and Carnival. Saus is definitely one of Panama's favorites.

Patties
(Empanadas)

Serves 6 to 8

Ingredients for Filling:

1 ½ pounds lean ground beef

1 large chopped onion

4 medium chopped green peppers

1 cup chopped parsley

1 cup chopped scallion

1 can (6 ounces) tomato paste

1 cup bread crumbs

1 minced garlic clove

1 teaspoon vinegar

2 cups water

1 teaspoon oregano

1 teaspoon thyme

½ teaspoon curry

Ají chombo or hot chile peppers to taste

Salt to taste

Ingredients for Dough:

12 cups flour

8 teaspoons salt

3 cups vegetable shortening or unsalted butter

2 ¼ cups cold water

Preparation:

Dough:

Mix flour with salt, and cut shortening into flour until mixture looks like coarse meal.

Add water to make dough and refrigerate about 1 hour.

Roll out the dough. With a 3 or 4-inch round biscuit cutter, cut out dough rounds to make empanada discs.

Filling:

Brown ground beef in a skillet over medium-low heat.

Add onion, green pepper, hot pepper, garlic, and all spices. Continue to cook over medium-low heat.

Add tomato paste and water; cook for 30 minutes.

Add bread crumbs; reduce heat and cook for 5 additional minutes. Remove beef and let cool.

Put 1 tablespoon of filling (don't over fill) on one side of empanada disc. Fold over to enclose filling and crimp edges with a fork or fingers to seal tightly. Repeat the process for each empanada disc.

Bake at 400°F 25 to 30 minutes, or until golden brown.

Bacalao Fritters
(Torrejitas de bacalao)

Serves 4 to 6

Ingredients:

1 cup bacalao (salted cod)

1 cup flour

½ cup water

1 teaspoon baking powder

¼ cup finely chopped onions

1 tablespoon scallion

1 seeded and chopped hot pepper

1 minced garlic clove

1 teaspoon paprika

½ teaspoon pepper

1 tablespoon parsley

Salt to taste

Canola oil (for frying)

Preparation:

Soak cod fish in cold water for 8 hours, or overnight.

Next day, change water at least three times; drain and boil for 10 minutes.

Cool, remove skin and bones and shred.

Put bacalao in a mixing bowl; add flour, baking powder, and salt. Mix well.

Add the rest of ingredients and mix well.

Heat oil in a skillet on medium heat; spoon mixture into hot oil.

Fry fritters until golden brown. Drain on paper towels and serve.

Chicken Empanadas
(Empanadas de pollo)

Serves 6 to 8

Ingredients for Filling:

1 pound skinless boneless chicken breast

1 cup chopped onion

½ cup chopped green peppers

½ cup chopped red peppers

1 cup chopped parsley

1 cup chopped scallion

1 tablespoon tomato paste

½ cup tomato sauce

2 minced garlic cloves

1 chicken bouillon cube

1 pack sazón with culantro (like La Flor or Goya)

1 teaspoon oregano

1 teaspoon thyme

1 cup water

Salt and pepper to taste

Canola oil

Ingredients for Dough:

1½ cups flour

3 tablespoons vegetable shortening or unsalted butter

3 cups cold water

1 teaspoon salt

Preparation:

Dough:

Mix flour with salt, and cut shortening into flour until the mix looks like coarse meal.

Add water to make dough and refrigerate about 1 hour.

Roll out the dough. With a 3 or 4-inch round biscuit cutter, cut out dough rounds to make empanada discs.

Filling:

Cook chicken in a skillet with water and chicken bouillon. Season to taste with salt and pepper. Cover and cook until chicken is done (reserve leftover liquid). Set aside to cool, shred and chop.

Heat oil in a skillet; add onion, peppers, garlic and fry 5 to 8 minutes. Then, add remaining spices and continue to cook.

Add tomato paste, tomato sauce, reserved liquid, and water. Mix and cook for 5 minutes.

Add chicken; reduce heat and cook for 5 additional minutes.

Remove chicken filling from heat and let cool.

Put 1 tablespoon of filling (don't over fill) on one side of empanada disc. Fold over to enclose filling and crimp edges with a fork or fingers to seal tightly. Repeat the process with each empanada disc.

Place empanadas on a greased or non-stick baking pan.

Bake at 400°F 20 to 25 minutes, or until golden brown.

Corn Dough for Empanadas
(Masa para empanadas de maíz)

Serves 10

Ingredients for Dough:

1 ½ cups yellow corn flour (like Goya Yellow Pre-Cooked Corn Meal)

4 tablespoons flour

1 tablespoon canola oil

2 cups water

1 tablespoon salt

Preparation:

Mix corn flour, flour, salt and oil; add water to make dough (add more or less water as necessary).

Grease your hands and pull out pieces of dough to make 3-inch round balls.

For filling ingredients and preparation, see previous recipe.

Fry or bake corn empanadas.

SALADS

Traditional Panamanian salads are comprised mostly of grains, starches, seafood, and cooked or raw fruits, vegetables, and roots. Panamanian salads usually include little or no green leafy vegetables. Lettuce, tomato, and watercress salads are the exception. The surge of foreign trained cooks and chefs have introduced a variety of green salads to restaurants. However, traditional salads are still preferred in most Panamanian homes.

Chayote Squash Salad
(Ensalada de chayote)

Serves 4 to 6

Ingredients:

4 chayote squash
2 chopped hard-boiled eggs
½ finely chopped small onion
¼ cup finely chopped celery
Mayonnaise to taste
Salt and pepper to taste

Preparation:

Wash, peel, and cube chayotes. Boil chayotes until tender. Drain water and let them cool.

In a bowl, mix everything together and refrigerate about 1 hour before serving.

TIPS: Look for chayotes that are firm and without bruises.

Panamanian-Style Potato Salad
(Ensalada de feria)

Serves 4 to 6

Ingredients:

4 potatoes with skin
2 medium beets with skin
2 eggs
1 finely chopped small onion
¼ cup finely chopped celery
½ tablespoon vinegar
Mayonnaise to taste
Salt and pepper to taste

Preparation:

Wash potatoes and beets to remove dirt. Boil potatoes and beets together.

In the last 10 minutes, add eggs to the water, then set aside to cool.

Shell eggs, peel potatoes and beets and cut them into cubes.

Refrigerate about 30 minutes.

In a bowl, mix everything together and refrigerate before serving.

CULTURAL NOTE: *This potato salad is usually served with rice and chicken. It is a popular dish at national and local fairs, parties, and celebrations.*

TIPS: *If potato salad is too dry add more mayonnaise.*

Avocado Salad
(Ensalada de aguacate)

Serves 4 to 6

Ingredients:

2 avocados
1 tomato
1 sliced large onion
¼ cup lime juice
¼ cup white vinegar
4 tablespoons olive oil
Salt and pepper to taste

Preparation:

Mix lime juice, vinegar, oil, salt, and pepper to make vinaigrette.

Slice avocados, tomato, and onion in rounds and arrange on a large plate.

Pour vinaigrette over salad and serve.

Avocado and Shrimp Salad
(Ensalada de aguacate y camarones)

Serves 4

Ingredients:

1 ripe avocado

1 pound fresh shrimp

1 chopped medium onion

4 seeded and chopped tomatoes

4 finely chopped garlic cloves

½ cup lime juice

½ teaspoon ground black pepper

2 teaspoons salt

½ cup olive oil

½ teaspoon oregano

2 chopped culantro leaves

Preparation:

Boil shrimp for 5 minutes; drain and peel. Place in mixing bowl.

In a separate bowl, mix lime juice, pepper, oregano, culantro, and salt to make vinaigrette. Set aside.

Peel avocado and cut into pieces; add avocado, onion, tomato, oil, and garlic to shrimp.

Pour vinaigrette over shrimp salad.

Mix well and serve.

Rice Salad
(Ensalada de arroz)

Serves 4 to 6

Ingredients:

2 cups cooked white rice

1 cup freshly grated carrots

½ cup minced onions

½ cup minced celery

½ cup chopped red bell pepper

½ cup chopped green bell pepper

Mayonnaise to taste

Salt and pepper to taste

Preparation:

Mix all ingredients together; refrigerate about 25 minutes and serve.

TIPS: It's a good way to use leftover rice.

Yuca Salad with Egg
(Ensalada de yuca con huevo)

Serves 8 to 10

Ingredients:

3½ pounds yuca

4 eggs

½ cup canola oil

1½ tablespoons dry parsley

Sea salt to taste

Pepper to taste

Preparation:

Wash and peel yuca (see tips).

Put yuca in a large pot with 4 quarts of water; add salt and boil yuca 35 to 40 minutes, or until soft. Drain and set aside to cool. Cut yuca into small cubes.

Boil eggs for about 10 minutes. Remove from stove and cover. Shell and cut hard-cooked eggs into small pieces.

In a mixing bowl, mix yuca, eggs, oil, and parsley; season to taste with salt and pepper.

Serve warm or cool.

TIPS: How to peel yuca root? With a paring knife, cut yuca into 3 to 4-inch pieces. Make a lengthwise slit in each piece. Pull off bark and under-skin. Cut each piece in half and remove the string from the middle.

Yuca Salad
(Ensalada de yuca)

Serves 8 to 10

Ingredients:

3½ pounds yuca

3 minced garlic cloves

1 cup chopped red onions

½ cup chopped fresh parsley

¼ teaspoon ground black pepper

¼ cup vinegar

¼ cup olive oil

Salt to taste

Preparation:

Follow preparation for yuca on previous recipe.

Heat oil in a skillet over low heat; lightly cook garlic, onion, parsley, and pepper. Remove promptly!

Pour mixture and vinegar over yuca; season to taste with salt. Mix well.

Serve warm or cool.

Green Papaya Salad

(Ensalada de papaya verde)

Serves 4

Ingredients:

1 medium green papaya

1 chopped small onion

2 eggs

½ cup vegetable or olive oil

½ cup vinegar

Salt and pepper to taste

Preparation:

Peel papaya and boil 3 to 4 minutes. Change the water and boil again on low heat until tender. Set aside to cool.

Boil eggs for 10 minutes. Remove from stove and cover. Shell and cut hard-cooked eggs into small cubes.

Cut papaya into small cubes and add all ingredients and mix well.

Carrot and Beet Salad
(Ensalada de zanahoria y remolacha)

Serves 4 to 6

Ingredients:

2 freshly grated large carrots

1 freshly grated large beet

Mayonnaise to taste

Salt and pepper to taste

Preparation:

Mix all the ingredients together and refrigerate about 25 minutes and serve.

CULTURAL NOTE: This is the original recipe of Eleanor Gale (Jiwanda's mother).

Bacalao Salad
(Ensalada de bacalao)

Serves 4

Ingredients:

1 pound good quality bacalao (Salted Cod Fish)

1 finely chopped medium onion

½ cup vegetable or olive oil

¼ cup vinegar

Pepper to taste

Preparation:

Soak salted cod in hot water for 1 hour. Drain water from cod, and soak for 8 hours in cool water. Remove cod from water and flake, making sure there are no bones.

Combine cod, onion, and the rest of ingredients.

Taste and refrigerate about 2 hours.

TIPS: *This salad is usually served over boiled potatoes and avocado.*

Elbow Macaroni Salad
(Ensalada de coditos)

Serves 4 to 6

Ingredients:

1 pound of elbow macaroni

½ pound cubed ham

Parsley to taste

Vinegar to taste

Mayonnaise to taste

Salt and pepper to taste

Preparation:

Cook macaroni al dente and strain. Set aside to cool.

Add all ingredients to macaroni and mix well.

Refrigerate about 1 hour before serving.

Pumpkin Salad
(Ensalada de zapallo)

Serves 4 to 6

Ingredients:

1 medium pumpkin (about 1½ pounds)

1 finely chopped large onion

2 finely chopped celery stalks

1½ cups chopped green bell peppers

2 eggs

Mayonnaise to taste

Salt and pepper to taste

Preparation:

Cut and peel pumpkin; remove seeds.

Boil pumpkin with salt until tender. Mash and set aside.

Boil eggs in a separate pot for 10 minutes. Remove from stove and cover. When cool, shell eggs and cut in rounds. Set aside.

Add the rest of ingredients and mix well. Garnish with egg rounds.

Refrigerate about 1 hour and serve.

Simple Watercress Salad
(Ensalada de berro)

Serves 4 to 6

Ingredients:

1 watercress bundle or ½ pound
Vinegar to taste
Salt and pepper to taste

Preparation

Wash watercress well, removing all impurities.

Place watercress in a bowl and add vinegar, salt, and pepper.

Toss and serve.

TIPS: *If watercress has too much of a peppery taste, just add lettuce and tomatoes to tone down the spicy flavor.*

SAUCES
AND
DRESSINGS

P anama is not really famous for its sauces and salad dressings; however, during our research we found out there is a fair selection of commercial brand Panamanian hot sauces. Yes, Panamanians like mild or hot sauces with their meals! It is not rare to find a hot sauce dispenser on the tables of restaurants and Panamanian homes. We gathered a few of the most popular and traditional homemade sauces and dressings made by our mothers, grandmothers, and friends. Most hot sauces used in Panama are heavily influenced by the Caribbean cuisine. The most traditional sauce appears to be the *salsa picante* or *Ají chombo sauce* brought to Panama by Antillean settlers. This sauce is used mostly to spice up soups, stews, beans, and meats. Other Panamanian sauces and dressings are a variation of recipes from residents of the former Canal Zone and from Panama's neighbors.

Coconut Dipping Sauce

(Salsa de coco)

Serves (varies)

Ingredients:

1 cup fresh coconut milk

½ cup fresh coconut flakes

2 cups milk

3 teaspoons cornstarch (or All-purpose flour)

2 teaspoons sugar

1 teaspoon cinnamon (optional)

Preparation:

Mix coconut milk and milk in a saucepan over medium heat until mixture starts to boil.

Add cornstarch or flour, one teaspoon at a time, until it starts to thicken slightly.

Add fresh coconut flakes and lower the heat.

Stir in the sugar and cinnamon until they blend in.

Did you know?

Coconut is a very important ingredient to indigenous cuisine: coconut water, coconut milk, and coconut sauces.

Panamanian Hot Sauce

(Salsa picante)

Serves (varies)

Ingredients:

6 Scotch bonnet peppers (Ají chombo or habanero)

6 yellow peppers (optional)

1 julienned large white onion

½ cup sugar

2 cups water

1 (32 ounces) clear glass sauce bottle (with plastic or metal cap)

Preparation:

Fill glass sauce bottle ½ full of water; add sugar and shake, until sugar is completely dissolved.

Cut peppers into two halves; place peppers with seeds and onion inside the bottle.

Put cap on bottle and wait 3 days before using sauce.

CULTURAL NOTE: *This traditional Panamanian-style hot sauce has just the right amount of spicy flavors to enhance the taste of all foods. It is a very versatile sauce because a few drops are great in or on just about everything: soups, stews, meats, salads, and much more. The recipe above is the original recipe of Juanita B. Lasso (Nilsa's grandmother). Today, variations of this sauce can be found at Latino supermarkets in the U.S. or it can be ordered online. We invite you to try our easy and natural original recipe.*

Ajilimójili Sauce
(Salsa ajilimójili)

Serves (varies)

Ingredients:

4 chile peppers

4 sweet peppers

1 teaspoon salt

4 peppercorns

5 garlic cloves

½ cup oil

¼ cup lemon juice

Preparation:

Grind up peppers, garlic, and peppercorns.

Season with salt and add oil and lemon juice.

Mix well and strain.

Honey and Lemon Juice Salad Dressing
(Aderezo de miel y limón)

Serves 2 to 4

Ingredients:

¼ cup honey

3 tablespoons fresh lemon juice

2 tablespoons apple cider vinegar or white vinegar

Preparation:

Heat honey for 5 seconds and blend with vinegar and lemon juice.

Panamanian-Style Chimichurri
(Chimichurri panameño)

Serves (varies)

Ingredients:

4 culantro leaves

4 garlic cloves

1 chopped large onion

4 seeded red peppers

2 seeded chile peppers

½ teaspoon ground cumin

¼ cup olive oil

Salt to taste

Preparation:

Mix all ingredients in a mixer or a food processor; process until smooth.

Sauce is served at room temperature. If sauce separates prior to serving, beat to combine.

Serve on the side with meat or vegetables.

CULTURAL NOTE: *It is believed that chimichurri sauce originated in Argentina and Uruguay. The gauchos (South American cowboys) have been using this sauce for their barbecues for many year. It is definitely a versatile sauce! This blend of natural ingredients is typically used as a marinade and dipping sauce for meats and sausages. It can also be added to grilled seafood, grilled vegetables, pasta sauces, and salads. Panamanians have given this sauce their own unique flavor. For instance, they add culantro which is considered a key ingredient in Panamanian cuisine. Panamanian-style chimichurri is often mixed with annatto oil and used to marinade and cook pork and chicken for tamales. This same mixture can also be used to sprinkle over while kneading dough for tamales to create a more colorful and flavorful dough.*

Vinaigrette Dressing

Serves 4

Ingredients:

¼ cup olive oil

2 tablespoons vinegar

2 tablespoons water

Salt and pepper to taste

Preparation:

Combine all ingredients in a small vinaigrette bottle and shake well before using.

Bocatoreña Tartar Sauce
(Salsa tártara bocatoreña)

Serves 4 to 6

Ingredients:

½ cup mayonnaise

2 teaspoons mustard

1 chopped small onion

1 chopped celery stalk

2 tablespoons fresh lemon juice

2 tablespoons water

Preparation:

Mix onion, celery, and water; place in glass mixing bowl.

Add the rest of ingredients and whisk to make a creamy smooth mixture.

Cover and refrigerate about 1 hour.

CULTURAL NOTE: Panamanians serve it with fish, salads, twice-fried plantains, fried yuca, and other fried dishes. It is also popular at special events, celebrations, birthdays, etc.

Tivoli Salad Dressing

(Aderezo estilo Tívoli)

Serves (varies)

Ingredients:

1 cup sugar

1 cup oil

1 cup apple cider vinegar

4 tablespoons catsup

½ minced garlic clove

1 medium finely chopped onion

¼ teaspoon dry mustard

Preparation:

Mix catsup, sugar, mustard, and garlic; add oil and whip until creamy.

Add vinegar and whip until the dressing is thick and creamy. Pour into a 2-quart glass container.

Add onion and refrigerate about 24 hours, or overnight.

CULTURAL NOTE: *This recipe is based on the original recipe from the Hotel Tivoli in the former Panama Canal Zone. The Tivoli (1905-1971) was built to provide accommodations to visitors, employees of de Canal, political dignitaries, and businessmen. The hotel became very popular among the locals, becoming a place for social gatherings and celebrations. The menu was designed to highlight the different areas along the Canal: "Tabernilla Pickles, Ancon Turtle, Mount Hope Olives, Corozal Potatoes, Culebra Fillet of Beef, Brazo Brooks Asparagus, La Boca Roast Turkey, Pedro Miguel Jelly, Potted Gatun Birds, Bas Obispo Punch, Cristobal, Balls, Matachin Ice Cream, Gorgona Cake, Colon Cheese, Empire Coffee, Cemetery Road Cigarettes and Las Cascadas Cigars" (Panamacanalmuseum.org).*

Sofrito

Serves (varies)

Ingredients:

1 medium onion

1 garlic bulb

1 green bell pepper

1 red pepper

2 large tomatoes

½ cup scallions

½ cup parsley

½ cup culantro

2 sweet peppers

1 Ají chombo or habanero pepper (optional)

¼ cup vinegar

¼ cup water

Preparation:

Mix all ingredients in a food processor or a blender.
Refrigerate.

SOUPS,
STEWS,
AND
ONE-POT MEALS

S oup is an important mainstay in Panama's everyday diet. Panamanian soups may be thin and clear, like Panamanian chicken, beef or fish broth; smooth and creamy, like some vegetable soups; thick and chunky, like *sancocho chiricano* and other soups made with meat, fish, seafood combination, grains, vegetables, and roots. Panamanians may serve soup as an appetizer, or as a first course in a meal. Typically, it is served as a hearty meal, especially at lunch. In our childhood, our mothers and grandmothers made soups or *sancochos* for lunch. We remember coming back from school and having a delicious hot bowl of soup. In Panama City and surrounding areas, *sancochos* and soups are similar. However, in the countryside there is a clear distinction between chicken soup and *sancocho*. In some rural areas there are variations of *sanchocho* recipes. Like in many other countries, soups, stews, and one-pot meals are popular in Panama. Traditionally, they are preferred by many because they are fast, easy, economical, and delicious. Let's not forget that these dishes are hearty and nutritious! It is customary to serve soups and stews with Ají chombo, a Panamanian hot sauce made with habanero peppers.

Chicken Sancocho

(Sancocho de pollo panameño)

Serves 6 to 8

Ingredients:

1 large chicken (approx. 2 ½ pounds)

1 chopped large onion

1 chopped green pepper

4 minced garlic cloves

4 chopped culantro leaves

1 packet chicken *consomé* (Maggi or Knorr)

1 tablespoon oregano

2 pounds ñame

2 chopped sweet red peppers

(or 2 red hot peppers)

Preparation:

Cut chicken in pieces; place in large pot of water and boil until chicken is done. Remove chicken and set aside (you can remove skin and bones if desired). Reserve water where chicken was boiled in.

Peel, wash, and cut ñame into 2-inch cubes.

Add chicken, onion, green pepper, garlic, and ñame to reserved water; add more water if necessary.

Cover pot and leave on medium heat until ñame is soft, but still firm.

Add culantro, chicken consomé, oregano, sweet or hot peppers, and salt to taste.

Reduce the heat and simmer for about 20 to 30 minutes.

Serve hot or warm with white rice.

CULTURAL NOTE: *While working on this cookbook, we became aware that in other parts of the nation there are clear differences between a regular chicken soup and the popular chicken sancocho. We interviewed cooks Aurora Gutiérrez and Olga Zoveida Ruiz from the central region (town of St. Augustine, Los Santos Province). According to them, the main ingredients of a true country-style sancocho are chicken, culantro and ñame. Regular chicken soup is chunkier because it has all the ingredients of the sancocho plus other vegetables, grains and/or roots. As one moves towards the Western region, the sanchocho appears to be heavier and thicker than sancochos prepared in any other parts of the country. For example, people from the province of Chiriqui add more vegetables, legumes, roots, and even grains (for example: yuca, otoe, squash, corn, etc.). It is said to be a good remedy for hangovers. In any case, sancocho is a "traditional chicken soup" and it is definitely one of Panama's favorites!*

TIPS: *In the countryside, a true sancocho is made with yard chicken. In the city, people buy what they call "gallina dura" (hormone free), when not available, broilers are used.*

NOTE: *Do not confuse ñame with yam. In the U.S., yam is really sweet potato and ñame is a long, round tuber with brown skin and off-white flesh. It has a creamy texture. Watch it! It might irritate your skin when in direct contact with creamy texture.*

Panamanian Broth

(Caldillo panameño)

Serves 8

Ingredients:

4 cups fish broth

1 pound crab

1 pound shrimp

½ teaspoon marjoram

1 tablespoon salt

1 small hot pepper

6 eggs

½ cup evaporated milk

¼ cup olive oil

2 cups chopped onion

1 cup chopped green peppers

5 minced garlic cloves

10 pear shaped tomatoes

1 can (6 ounces) tomato paste

Preparation:

Clean and chop shrimp and crab. Make broth with shells, enough to make 4 cups. Set aside.

Heat oil in pot on medium-low; cook and stir the onion, green peppers, and garlic lightly.

Remove seeds from tomatoes and chop; add to mix.

Stir and add tomato paste and broth. Let boil for 20 minutes. Add chopped crab, shrimp, marjoram, hot pepper, and salt. Let boil on low heat for 15 minutes. Remove broth from heat. Mix eggs and add 1 tablespoon broth. Pour egg mix slowly to pot and leave covered for 7 minutes.

Pour milk in a large bowl and pour broth over the milk.

Cow Foot Soup

(Sopa de pata de res)

Serves 4 to 6

Ingredients:

1 cow leg (use pre-cut beef bones from lower leg)

2 pounds yuca

2 pounds ñame

2 pounds otoe

1 tablespoon lime juice

1 chopped onion

3 chopped garlic cloves

6 finely chopped tomatoes

3 chopped culantro leaves

2 chopped green peppers

1 teaspoon dry oregano

1 tablespoon salt

Preparation:

Clean beef bones. Place beef bones and root vegetables in a large pot with water.

Add lime juice and boil; cover and cook for 45 minutes and skim the soup.

Add the onion, garlic, tomatoes, culantro, and peppers.

Let it cook until meat is tender.

Add oregano and salt (add more salt, if desired).

Serve warm.

One Pot

Serves 8 to 10

Ingredients:

6 cups rice

1 ½ pounds codfish

1 ½ pounds shrimp

2 pounds pig tails

1 pound fresh grated coconut

1 chopped large onion

3 chopped large green peppers

1 cup chopped scallion (green onion)

1 cup chopped fresh parsley

1 teaspoon oregano

Salt and pepper to taste

Vegetable or olive oil

Preparation:

Soak salted cod in hot water for an hour. Drain water from cod; soak for 8 additional hours in cool water.

Remove skin and bones and chop into small pieces.

Chop pig tails into small pieces and cook until soft.

Wash shrimp and set aside.

Extract about 8 cups coconut milk (see tips for "Rice with Coconut" recipe).

Stir-fry onion, green peppers, scallion, and parsley in a small amount of oil until tender.

Add codfish, pig tails, shrimp, oregano, salt, pepper, and coconut milk. Boil for about 20 minutes.

Reduce heat and add rice; cover and let cook until done.

CULTURAL NOTE: *This recipe is based on the original recipe of Afro-Panamanians from the province of Bocas del Toro whose ancestors came from the West Indies.*

Oxtail Soup
(Sopa de rabo de buey)

Serves 8 to 10

2½ pounds pre-cut oxtail
2 peeled medium potatoes cut into small cubes
4 cups beef stock
1 cup water
3 minced garlic cloves
1 chopped medium onion
1 tablespoon fresh thyme
2 tablespoons sea salt

Preparation:

Trim excess fat from around oxtail pieces and place in a slow cooker.

Add beef stock, water, garlic, and salt. Cook on low for 8 hours, or overnight.

Next day, remove bones and skim fat from top of the soup surface.

Add potatoes; cover and cook for 25 minutes.

Add the rest of ingredients and cook 15 to 20 minutes.

Serve hot or warm and enjoy!

Mondongo

Serves 8 to 10

Ingredients:

2 pounds chopped tripe

¼ cup canola oil

½ cup chopped green pepper

1 cup chopped onion

4 minced garlic cloves

1 can (8 ounces) tomato sauce

1½ pounds yuca

1½ pounds potatoes

1 Ají chombo or Scotch bonnet

2 teaspoons salt

Preparation:

Wash tripe thoroughly in hot water and cut into 3 x 1 inch strips.

Cook tripe in enough water until soft.

Peel and cut yuca and potatoes into small pieces; add to tripe and cook until yuca and potatoes are both soft.

Heat oil in a skillet and cook and stir onion, green peppers, ají chombo, and garlic; add tomato sauce and salt.

Add this mixture to tripe and cook on low heat 15 to 20 minutes, or until broth thickens.

Serve with white rice.

CULTURAL NOTE: This is a traditional Panamanian dish, also known as Mondongo Criollo (Creole Tripe). In Mexico, it's known as Menudo. This Mexican dish is made with beef stomach in a clear broth or with a red chili base (Menudo Colorado). In Mexico, people cut larger pieces of tripe and it is usually served with tortillas or other breads. In Panama, mondongo is cut in smaller pieces and it is typically served with white rice.

Guacho

Serves 10 to 12

Ingredients:

1 pound red beans

2 cups rice

1½ pounds cubed salt pork

1 pound yuca

1 pound ñame

Salt and pepper to taste

Preparation for Guacho:

Wash beans. In a slow cooker, cook beans and salt pork on low 6 to 8 hours, or overnight.

Next day, add rice, mixing well with beans and meat.

Peel and cut yuca and ñame into small pieces and cook until tender.

Refrito:

While the guacho is cooking, lightly fry the vegetables and tomato paste. Put a big tablespoonful of "refrito" on top of each serving of guacho.

Ingredients for the refrito:

1 chopped sweet pepper

1 chopped medium onion

1 chopped stalk celery

4 minced garlic cloves

1 can (6 ounces) tomato paste

Salt and pepper to taste

Spotted Rooster
(Gallo pinto)

Serves 6 to 8

Ingredients:

1 pound pinto beans

1 cup rice

1 pound diced lean pork or beef

½ pound salted pig tails (cut in small pieces)

1½ pounds diced yuca

2 cups chopped hot peppers

1 chopped large onion

3 garlic cloves

3 finely chopped culantro leaves

10 diced roma tomatoes

1 can (12 ounces) peeled tomatoes

1 tablespoon vinegar

1 seeded and chopped habanero pepper

½ cup canola oil

Salt to taste

Preparation:

Wash beans and soak for 8 hours, or overnight. Drain.

In a large pot, add water, pig tails and beans and cook until tender.

In another 6-quart pot put lean pork to cook in a cup of water until tender; add yuca and continue to cook on low.

Heat oil in a 4-quart skillet and cook and stir onion, hot peppers, and garlic.

Add culantro, tomatoes and simmer for 3 minutes; add roma tomatoes, vinegar, and habanero pepper. Cook for 5 additional minutes and reserve sauce.

Add beans and pig tails to pork and yuca; add rice, salt, and water if needed. When rice is almost done, add half reserved tomato sauce; cook rice until tender.

Serve the spotted rooster with the rest of tomato sauce.

CULTURAL NOTE: A hearty breakfast of "Caribbean porridge" made of rice, beans, and pork, is called gallo pinto, or spotted rooster, and can be found in local establishments. Interestingly, gallo pinto is a traditional dish in Costa Rican and Nicaraguan cuisine but varies from country to country.

NOTE: Can be served with fried green plantains (patacones) or fried ripe plantains.

Pigeon Soup
(Sopa de paloma)

Serves 4

Ingredients:

2 pigeons

6 cups water

1 sliced onion

1 minced garlic clove

2 pounds cubed ñame

¼ cup rice

Salt to taste

Preparation:

Clean and cut pigeon in halves; add water, onion, and garlic. Let stand for 30 minutes.

Cook on medium-low heat until it boils. Simmer, uncovered, until pigeon is tender.

Add rice, ñame, and season to taste with salt; cook until rice and ñame are done.

Salpreso Soup

Serves 4 to 6

Ingredients:

3 whole cleaned dried and salted swordfish

8 julienned sweet peppers

1 julienned large onion

4 minced garlic cloves

2 pounds cubed ñame

1 tablespoon oregano

8 chopped culantro leaves

1 teaspoon pepper

1 teaspoon annatto oil

Salt to taste

Preparation:

Put fish in water for 5 hours. Wash and set aside.

In a medium pot, cook and stir onion, garlic, sweet pepper, and oregano with annatto oil for 5 minutes to make sauce. Remove and set aside.

Fill same pot ½ full of water and bring it to a boil; add ñame and cook until soft.

Add sauce, salt to taste, and fish.

Simmer, uncovered, 10 to 15 minutes.

Serve hot or warm.

CUTURAL NOTE: Traditionally, in rural areas, especially in the province of Veraguas, people buy the whole fish and preserve it with salt to make salpreso soup. They put the fish out in the sun to dry for several days. In other areas people may dry the fish by hanging it from metal racks over a fogón (a cooking area or a rustic stove, usually constructed of bricks or stones. A fogón is commonly used in true rural and traditional Panamanian kitchens).

TIPS: Dried and salted fish can be purchased at specialty stores or online.

Fish Head Broth
(Sopa de cabeza de pescado)

Serves 4

Ingredients:

4 fried fish heads

1 pound cubed ñame

1 green or red pepper

1 chopped medium onion

1 julienned large tomato

2 chopped culantro leaves

5 cups water

Salt, pepper and hot sauce to taste

Preparation:

Boil fish heads in medium pot. Add all ingredients, except ñame. Let boil over medium-low heat for about 1 hour.

Remove heads and crushed them well. Strain and boil broth for 10 minutes.

Add ñame and let cook until soft.

Serve hot or warm with white rice.

Seafood Combination Soup
(Sopa criolla de mariscos)

Serves 6 to 8

Ingredients:

2 pounds fresh fish fillets (cod, flounder or sea bass)

1 pound fresh shelled and deveined large shrimp

¾ pound mussels (about 12)

2 pounds cubed ñame

1 chopped green pepper

1 chopped medium onion

1 julienned large tomato

3 chopped culantro leaves

6 cups water

1 large lemon

Salt, pepper and hot sauce to taste

Preparation:

Wash and cut fish fillets into 1-inch pieces; add lemon juice.

Just before cooking, soak mussels for 20 minutes. Make sure mussels are well scrubbed and beards removed.

In a large pot, combine all ingredients, except ñame, mussels and shrimp.

Add water and let boil over medium-low heat 15 to 20 minutes.

Add ñame and let it cook until soft.

Add shrimp and mussels. Cover and cook over low heat for an additional 10 minutes, or until mussels have opened. Be careful not to cook shrimp and mussels too long or they will become tough and grainy.

Serve hot or warm with white rice.

Rice and Seafood Stew
(Guacho de marisco)

Serves 10 to 12

Ingredients:

2 pounds clams

2 pounds squid

2 pounds shrimp

2 lobsters

1 pound scallops

4 cups rice

½ cup olive oil

1 cup chopped onions

½ cup chopped green peppers

4 minced garlic cloves

2 cups chopped pear tomatoes

2 bay leaves

3 chopped culantro leaves

1 hot pepper

1½ cups red wine

10 cups water

1 tablespoon salt

Preparation:

In a large skillet, stir and cook onions, green peppers, and garlic; add tomatoes and cook for 5 minutes, while mixing.

Add culantro, hot pepper, bay leaves, and wine.

Clean and cut clams, squid, shrimp, and lobster into small pieces; add all seafood, including scallops to sauce in skillet. Add water and boil over medium-low heat for 10 minutes.

Wash rice and add it to ingredients in skillet. Season with salt (add more salt, if desired).

Mix everything together, cover and cook over low heat, until rice is done.

Shrimp Stew
(Chupe de camarones)

Serves 4 to 6

Ingredients:

2 pounds shrimp

¼ cup canola oil

1 chopped medium onion

1 chopped green pepper

1 can (12 ounces) peeled tomatoes

¼ cup white wine

2 teaspoons salt

2 chopped culantro leaves

2 pounds peeled and cubed potatoes

4 cups water

Preparation:

Peel and clean shrimp.

Cook and stir onion and pepper with oil in deep skillet.

Add tomatoes and mash them with cooking spoon; let cook 2 to 3 minutes and add wine, salt, culantro, potatoes, and water.

Cook for 20 minutes.

Add shrimp and cook for no more than 10 minutes.

Serve hot with hot pepper sauce on the side, if desired.

Callaloo Soup with Eggs
(Sopa de kalalú con huevos)

Serves 4 to 6

Ingredients:

6 callaloo leaves

4 eggs

2 pounds yuca

2 pounds ñame

2 pounds otoe

1 medium onion

4 culantro leaves

4 sweet peppers

2 tablets chicken flavor bouillon

2 cups chicken broth

8 cups water

Salt to taste

Preparation:

Boil callaloo leaves until soft.

Peel root vegetables; cook in 8 cups of water 45 to 50 minutes, or until soft. Chop onion, culantro, and peppers and add to soup.

Add tablets, broth, and salt to taste.

Beat eggs and add to soup; cook until thickens.

English-Style Coconut Soup
(Sopa de coco inglesa)

Serves 6

Ingredients:

2 quarts chicken or vegetable stock

½ pound grated fresh coconut

2 ounces rice flour

2 tablespoons of cream

Salt, mace and pepper to taste

Preparation:

Soak grated coconut in a little stock and extract milk. Set aside.

Boil stock; add a small blade of mace and coconut milk. Simmer for about 1 hour.

Mix rice flour smoothly with some stock; boil remainder stock, add blended rice flour.

Stir and boil gently for about 10 minutes.

Season to taste with salt and pepper.

Stir in the cream and serve.

Soup with Cafongo

Serves 4

Ingredients:

2 pounds beef (chuck cubes)

2 chopped culantro leaves

1 pound ñame

2 pounds yuca

2 pounds otoe

1 green plantain

5 ears of corn

½ pound creole or sweet pepper (ají criollo)

1 minced garlic clove

Canola oil

Cafongo Preparation:

Shuck corn (see tips for "Corn Fritters" recipe). Grind corn with one culantro leaf and a dash of salt to make a mix.

Soup Preparation:

Peel and cut plantain into rounds.

Heat one tablespoon of oil in large pot; add meat, one culantro leaf, and plantain.

When meat is browned, add enough water to cover meat and about two additional cups of water.

Simmer for 1 hour, or until meat is tender; add yuca and cook for 5 minutes.

Add otoe and ñame. Simmer until root vegetables are tender.

Spoon cafongos into soup and simmer for a few minutes.

Serve hot.

VARIATION: Use one pound of beef ribs instead of the chuck. Make the cafongo dough with two boiled plantains (one green and one medium ripe). Mash both with a refrito of annatto oil, onion, garlic, and sweet pepper. Make little balls, and add to soup.

RICE

According to The Cambridge World History of Food, rice is "a member of the grass family (*Gramineae*) and belongs to the genus *Oryza* under tribe Oryzeae. The genus *Oryza* includes 20 wild species and 2 cultivated species. The wild species are widely distributed in the humid tropics and subtropics of Africa, Asia, Central and South America, and Australia. Of the two cultivated species, African rice (*O. glaberrima* Steud.) is confined to West Africa, whereas common or Asian rice (*O. sativa* L.) is now commercially grown in 112 countries..." (Kiple and Coneè Ornelas). Asian rice is the most popular in Panama. It is used as a main dish, mixed with chicken, pork, seafood, fruit, beans, vegetable or a combination of some of these ingredients. It can also be served plain as a side dish. It is used as the main ingredient for some desserts and drinks. In the rural areas, rice is sometimes served as part of an early morning breakfast, especially among farmers. Its popularity is such that Panamanians have the following saying "You have not eaten yet, if you have not had rice."

Rice desserts and drinks can be found under **DESSERTS AND SWEETS** and **JUICES, DRINKS, AND SHAKES**, respectively.

Fututiado Rice

(Arroz fututiado)

Serves 16

Ingredients:

4 cups new rice or white rice

Salt to taste

Preparation:

Wash rice and in a heated 4-quart pot, toast it. When rice is toasted, let cool and save for other recipes or cook immediately (for cooking instructions see "Panamanian-Style White Rice" recipe).

CULTURAL NOTES: The method used for this recipe mimics the one used to dry new rice after the last harvest was completed.

Panamanian-Style White Rice
(Arroz Blanco)

Serves 8

Ingredients:

2 cups white rice

4 cups water

½ finely chopped medium onion

Canola oil

Salt to taste

Preparation:

Wash rice to remove some of the starch.

Heat oil in a 2-quart pot and add rice; fry rice for 10 minutes, making sure it does not burn.

When rice is bright white, add onion, water, and salt.

Cover and simmer until tender.

CUTURAL NOTE: Cooking rice in a thick cast iron pot (or paila) is the most traditional way of cooking rice in Panama, especially in the rural areas.

VARIATION: Add all ingredients in the pot (onion is optional). Cover and simmer, checking that the rice is cooked.
TIPS: If rice burns, cut an onion in halves and put inside. Cover and keep at a low heat until the odor disappears.

Chicken with Rice
(Arroz con pollo)

Serves 16

Ingredients:

3 cups white rice

1 whole chicken cut in pieces (3 pounds)

2 packs sazón (like La Flor or Goya)

1 cup diced green peppers

1 cup diced red bell peppers

1 (10 ounces) frozen pack of peas and carrots

½ cup chopped olives

¼ cup cappers

1 cup finely chopped onions

3 garlic cloves

4 tablespoons canola oil

2 tablespoons tomato paste

1 tablespoon salt

2½ cups chicken stock

2 cups water

Black pepper to taste

Preparation:

Season chicken with salt, black pepper, and 1 minced garlic clove; let marinate 30 to 45 minutes.

Heat oil in a 12-inch skillet, place chicken skin side down and lightly brown on both sides. Remove chicken from skillet and set aside.

Cook and stir onion, garlic, green and red peppers in the same skillet until tender.

Dissolve tomato paste in about ½ cup water.

Add chicken and tomato paste to other ingredients. Cover and simmer until done. Remove chicken from sauce and let cool. Reserve sauce.

Debone and shred chicken.

In a pot, add rice, chicken, chicken stock, water, sazón, and reserved sauce (taste water and add salt if necessary). Simmer, uncovered, until most of the water is absorbed.

Add the rest of vegetables. Mix, cover, and cook on low until done.

TIPS: If rice is not cooking evenly, make few holes in rice and add a small amount of water. Then, put a piece of wax paper over the rice and cover tightly.

NOTE: If available substitute the sazón with culantro and annatto oil. Cook and stir culantro and annatto oil, before adding rice.

Rice with Coconut

(Arroz con coco)

Serves 8

Ingredients:

2 cups white rice

4 cups fresh coconut milk

Salt to taste

Preparation

In a 2-quart pot bring coconut milk to a boil (see tips); add the rest of ingredients.

Mix, cover, and cook on low 20 to 30 minutes, or until rice is tender.

How to shell a coconut? *Preheat oven to 325°F. Pierce the end of the coconut with a nail to open a hole into one of the eyes of the coconut. Drain the coconut water into a bowl. Hold the thickest part of the coconut firmly on a hard surface. The eyes must be pointing left or right. Hit the center of the coconut with the blunt side of a large knife, producing a crack in the shell. Rotate the coconut and continue hitting the center until the crack has completed the circumference of the nut. Break the nut into smaller pieces using your hands. Remove the meat from the husk with a flexible knife.*

CULTURAL NOTE: *This recipe is usually served with seafood in the coastal areas of the province of Colon and in some areas of the province of Panama.*

TIPS: *To make fresh coconut milk, grate coconut and add 4 cups of warm water. Soak grated coconut in water and extract milk.*

Rice and Beans with Coconut
(Arroz con frijoles)

Serves 12

Ingredients:

2 cups white rice

4 cups fresh coconut milk

1½ cups kidney beans or 1 can (15 ounces) kidney beans

1 tablespoon finely chopped fresh thyme

2 tablespoons canola oil

Salt to taste

Preparation:

Heat oil in a 2-quart pot, add rice and stir for 10 minutes, making sure it does not burn. Add the rest of ingredients. If using dry kidney beans, see tips.

Mix, cover, and cook on low 20 to 30 minutes, or until rice is tender.

TIPS: The can of beans can be substituted with dry beans. Soak beans overnight or 8-10 hours and then cook until soft, but still firm. See tips on how to peel coconut and how to extract coconut milk on previous recipe.
You can substitute fresh coconut milk with 1 can (13.5 ounces) coconut milk; mix with 2 cups water.

All-In-One

Serves 10

Ingredients:

3 cups white rice

4 cups fresh coconut milk

1 pound bacalao (Salted Cod Fish)

2 onces small dried shrimp

1 pig tail (8 inches)

14 ounces frozen pigeon peas

3 tablespoons annatto oil

1 finely chopped medium onion

1 cup water

Canola oil

Salt to taste

Preparation:

Soak salted cod in hot water for an hour; drain and soak in cool water again for 8 hours, or overnight.

Next day, soak dried shrimp and clean any impurities or shells.

Drain water from cod and flake, making sure there are no bones.

Heat oil in a large 4–quart pot; add shrimp, cod fish, and onion.

Cook and stir ingredients for 10 minutes.

In another pot, add pig tail pieces and 1 cup water. Cover and cook on medium-high for 10 minutes.

Add coconut milk, rice, pigeon peas, annatto oil, pig tail to shrimp and cod mixture (see tips on how to make coconut milk under "Rice with Coconut" recipe).

Taste for salt, cover, and simmer on low for 30 minutes, or until done.

CULTURAL NOTE: This is the original recipe of Eleanor Gale (Jiwanda's mother). She got it from her mother who was a Panamanian of Afro-Caribbean descent. This rice recipe is usually served during Christmas and New Year celebrations.

TIPS: How to make Annatto oil?
1 cup of oil
2 tablespoons annatto seeds. Heat oil and add annatto seeds, until oil turns bright red. Leave to cool, strain and discard seeds. Store unused annatto oil.

Rice with Green Pigeon Peas and Coconut
(Arroz con guandú y coco)

Serves 6

Ingredients:

2 cups white rice

1 can (13.5 ounces) coconut milk or 4 cups fresh coconut milk

14 ounces frozen pigeon peas or 1 can (15 ounces) of pigeon peas

Salt to taste

Preparation:

In a 2-quart pot bring coconut milk to a boil (see tips under "Rice with Coconut" recipe).

Add the rest of ingredients.

Mix, cover, and cook on low 20 to 30 minutes, or until rice is tender.

CULTURAL NOTE: This recipe is better known as "Rice with Coconut and Gungu Pea" by Panamanians of Afro-Caribbean descent.

Rice with Coconut and Dried Small Shrimp
(Arroz con coco y camaroncitos)

Serves 4 to 6

Ingredients:

2 cups white rice

8 ounces dried small shrimp

4 cups of fresh coconut milk

Salt to taste

Preparation:

Soak and clean shrimp thoroughly.

Cook shrimp in coconut milk for 10 minutes on medium-high (see tips under "Rice with Coconut" recipe).

Add the rest of ingredients, cover, and cook on low 20 to 30 minutes, or until rice is tender.

TIPS: Add a teaspoon of sugar to coconut to enhance the flavor.

Rice with Pork
(Arroz con puerco)

Serves 6 to 8

Ingredients:

2 cups white rice

3 cups water

1 chopped small onion

4 minced garlic cloves

½ pound chopped pork

2 large red bell peppers

4 finely chopped celery stalks

4 chopped green onions

1 (2 ounces) jar alcaparrado (like Goya Alcaparrado)

2 tablespoons canola oil

1 package of banana leaves

Salt to taste

Preparation:

Place chopped pork in a heated large saucepan; add enough water to cover pork, let it dry and brown in own fat.

Add vegetables, *alcaparrado*, and garlic to pork. Cover and simmer on medium-high for 10 minutes, drain and reserve pork stock in a separate bowl.

Heat oil in a 4-quart pot and add rice, stir for 10 minutes, making sure it does not burn.

Add reserved pork stock to rice. Mix, cover, and cook on medium-high for 20 minutes.

Add pork mixture and cook on low 10 to 20 minutes, or until rice is completely cooked.

For best results, cover rice with banana leaves when cooking.

Alcaparrado
Olives, cappers, and pimento peppers in brine.

TIPS: *Heat diffusers are very useful for even cooking, especially when cooking rice.*

Rice with Crab
(Arroz con cangrejo)

Serves 4

Ingredients:

1½ cups white rice

2 cups water

4 large crabs

1 chopped medium onion

2 chopped medium red bell peppers

2 chopped medium tomatoes

2 chopped culantro leaves

4 tablespoons canola oil

Salt to taste

Preparation:

Boil or steam crabs until they turn red. Remove crab meat and discard shells, set aside.

Heat oil in a large 4-quart skillet, cook and stir onion, peppers, tomatoes, culantro, and crab meat for 5 minutes; add 2 cups of water and simmer for 15 minutes.

Add rice and salt to taste. Mix, cover, and cook on low until rice is done.

Culantro leaves*, also known as recaito or recao verde.*

Rice with Jumbo Shrimp
(Arroz con langostino)

Serves 8 to 10

Ingredients:

3 cups rice

1 pound peeled and deveined large shrimp

½ cup canola oil

1 cup finely chopped onion

1 cup finely chopped green peppers

4 chopped garlic cloves

½ teaspoon ground black pepper

1 can (6 ounces) tomato paste

3 cups water

2 cups beer (your favorite)

1 teaspoon salt

Preparation:

Cook and stir onion, green pepper, and garlic; add black pepper, tomato paste and mix.

Add shrimp and water. When it starts boiling, add rice and salt. Cover and cook 15 to 20 minutes.

Add beer and cook for 5 additional minutes, or until rice is done.

Rice with Clams
(Arroz con almejas)

Serves 8 to 10

Ingredients:

3 cups rice

2 pounds cleaned unshelled clams

¼ cup canola oil

1 finely chopped large onion

1 finely chopped green pepper

1 finely chopped red pepper

2 finely chopped garlic cloves

1 can (12 ounces) peeled tomatoes

½ teaspoon ground black pepper

2 teaspoons salt

3 cups water

Preparation:

Cook and stir onion, green pepper, and garlic; add tomatoes, black pepper, and salt.

Add clams and rice; mix well and add water. Cook until rice is done.

Serve warm with red peppers over the top.

Rice with Squid

(Arroz con calamares)

Serves 4 to 6

Ingredients:

2 cups rice

2 pounds cleaned squid

1 chopped green sweet pepper

1 chopped red sweet pepper

1 chopped large onion

1 minced garlic clove

2 seeded and chopped tomatoes

4 tablespoons canola oil

4 cups water

1 ½ teaspoons saffron,

Salt and ground black pepper to taste

Preparation:

Heat 2 tablespoons oil in a frying pan; cut squid into small pieces and cook 4 to 5 minutes. Remove and set aside.

Cook and stir onion until golden; add peppers, tomato, salt, and black pepper. Cook over low heat. When mixture thickens, add squid.

Pour the remaining 2 tablespoons of oil in a heavy bottomed pan with a close fitting lid. Lightly fry rice and garlic, until golden.

Add squid and vegetable mixture to rice. Cook for 2 minutes and then add water and saffron. Bring to a boil and cover tightly.

Simmer over low heat 10 to 15 minutes, or until rice is done and water is absorbed.

Home-Style Panamanian Fried Rice
(Arroz frito chino)

Serves 4 to 6

Ingredients:

2 cups cooked white rice

1 finely chopped medium onion

1 cup coarsely grated carrot

1 finely chopped celery stalk

2 cups shredded green cabbage

1 cup cooked chopped chicken or beef

2 beaten eggs (optional)

Chopped green onion (optional)

Canola oil

Soy sauce to taste

Preparation:

Heat oil in a large 4-quart skillet, cook and stir cabbage, celery, carrot, and onion until soft; add meat to rice.

Fry rice, add eggs and mix well.

Add soy sauce to rice, turning to brown evenly.

Garnish with green onion and serve.

CULTURAL NOTE: *This recipe highlights the Chinese influence in Panama where soy sauce is also known as "salsa china" (Chinese sauce).*

Rice with Pumpkin
(Arroz con zapallo)

Serves 4 to 6

Ingredients:

2 cups white rice

2 cups cubed pumpkin

1 finely chopped small onion

3½ cups water

3 tablespoons canola oil

Salt to taste

Preparation:

In a 2-quart pot, cook and stir onion and pumpkin until onion is transparent.

Add water and bring to a boil for about 10 minutes.

Add rice and season to taste with salt.

Mix, cover, and cook on low until rice is tender.

TIPS: *Substitute 1 cup water with 1 cup fresh coconut milk to enhance the flavor. See tips on how to extract coconut milk under "Rice and Coconut" recipe.*

Rice with Bacalao
(Arroz con bacalao)

Serves 6

Ingredients:

2 cups white rice

3 cups water

1 pound bacalao

2 minced garlic cloves

1 finely chopped large onion

1½ cups chopped green and red bell peppers

1 can (12 ounces) chopped tomatoes

¼ teaspoon thyme

1 parsley branch

4 tablespoons canola oil

Preparation:

Soak salted cod in hot water for an hour; drain and soak in cool water again for 8 hours, or overnight.

Drain water from cod and flake, making sure there are no bones.

In a large 4-quart skillet, heat 2 tablespoons oil and stir onion, peppers, and garlic. Fry for 5 minutes and add tomatoes, thyme, and parley; add bacalao to the mix.

In a separate 4-quart pot, lightly fry rice with 2 tablespoons oil for 5 minutes.

Add water to rice and boil, uncovered, on medium heat until most of the water is absorbed; add bacalao mix.

Mix, cover, and cook on low until rice is fully cooked.

Rice with Burgao
(Arroz con burgao)

Serves 4

Rice ingredients:

2 cups rice

The milk of one grated coconut

Burgao ingredients:

2½ pounds burgao (sea snails)

2 chopped culantro leaves

2 large chopped green peppers

2 minced garlic cloves

1/8 teaspoon oregano

1 pack sazón with annatto (like La Flor or Goya)

1 can (14 ounces) coconut

The milk of one grated coconut

Rice preparation:

Soak grated coconut in three cups of warm water and extract milk.

In a pot add coconut milk and rice. Cover and cook for 20 minutes or until rice is tender.

Burgao preparation:

Take burgao out of the shell, including tail. Put burgao to boil for one hour, depending on the size

When burgao is soft add all ingredients. Cook until it becomes a stew.

Mix with rice; cover and cook on low for 5 minutes and serve.

Panamanian Paella
(Paella estilo panameño)

Serves 10 to 12

Ingredients:

5 cups cooked rice
3 pounds chicken
3 pounds cubed lean pork (optional)
1 large lobster
1 pound squid
1 pound shrimp
2½ pounds clams
3 pounds national chorizo
½ pound razor clam
½ pound mussels
4 chopped onions
4 finely chopped green peppers
3 minced garlic cloves
3 seeded cubed medium tomatoes
1 can (6 ounces) tomato paste
1 can (14 ounces) tomato sauce
1 can (15 ounces) green peas (baby green peas or chickpeas)
¼ cup chopped fresh parsley
¼ cup chopped fresh scallions
6 tablespoons vegetable or olive oil
1 cup stuffed green Spanish olives
1 cup water
Salt and pepper to taste

Preparation:

Wash rice well and in a large deep pot (or a paella pan), put oil and fry rice. Set aside.

Cut and fry chicken well; cool and debone. Set aside

Make a sauce with onion, garlic, green pepper, tomato, tomato sauce, and tomato paste; add water and cook over low heat 8 to 10 minutes.

Separately, fry chorizo in small pieces and do the same with pork.

Boil lobsters and shrimp and peel them.

Clean and slice clams and squid.

Separately, cook clams with scallions and parsley. Add about 5 cups of the liquid seafood was cooked in.

Add chorizo, chicken, pork, whole shrimp, small lobster pieces, clams, squid, and mussels to rice. Also add sauce, peas, and olives; mix well.

Cook over medium heat for 10 minutes. Cover and simmer over low heat for 45 minutes.

CULTURAL NOTE: *There are various types of paella (Valencian paella, seafood paella, and mixed paella); one of the most widely known seems to be the Velencian paella from Valencia, Spain where it's believed to have originated from (around the mid-nineteenth century). Basically, it is a rice dish with different kinds of meats, seafood, and vegetables. It is worth noting that originally seafood was not one of the* *main ingredients. In the past, paella was a popular meal among low-income people. Traditionally, it is cooked in large quantities in a shallow pan (or paellera) made of carbon steel. According to the Paella Company, "it was cooked over an open fire in the fields and eaten directly from the pan using wooden spoons. Seafood is rare in the fields of Valencia, which is why they used chicken, rabbit, duck, and snails." Making paella was and still is a laborious task, but it's so worth it. Today, paella can be very pricey, but it is still a popular dish around the world. This delicious dish was brought to Panama by Spaniards. It is available at exclusive Panamanian restaurants. Panamanian families also make it for special occasions, such as local festivals, birthdays, and other special social gatherings.*

CORN

Panamanians eat corn in a variety of ways: deep-fried tortillas, large and thick corn cake tortillas, empanadas, tamales, corn fritters, *bollos* (thick corn meal or fresh corn paste wrapped in corn husks, corn leaves, Royal Palm tree leaves, sugar cane leaves, banana or plantain leaves), corn cereal, breads, soups, and a variety of drinks and alcoholic beverages, such as, chicheme, hamony, and *chichas fuertes* (popular fermented corn drinks). Corn is definitely a popular ingredient among Panamanians. This does not come as a surprise, since natives of the Americas were growing corn extensively long before the arrival of the Europeans. It is said that the probable center of origin of "corn" is the Central American and Mexican regions. Maize flour has been important in Mesoamerican cuisine since ancient times, and remains a staple in much of Latin American cuisine. Mesoamerica refers to a geographical region of similar cultures, comprising most of Central America and a large area of Mexico.

Corn breads and corn drinks can be found under **BREADS, JUICES, DRINKS, AND SHAKES**, and **ALCOHOLIC BEVERAGES**, respectively.

Wrapped Tamales
(Tamales panameños)

Serves 15 to 20

Ingredients:

2 ½ pounds cracked corn

2 pounds cubed lean pork (1 ½ -inch cubes)

2 pounds cut boneless chicken (2-inch pieces)

2/3 cup canola oil

2 cups annatto oil

3 cups chopped onions

7 garlic cloves

½ cup chopped green peppers

½ cup chopped red peppers

1 tablespoon sea salt

5 large culantro leaves

4 cups water

1 cup prunes and/or raisins

1 cup stuffed Spanish olives

20 faldo leaves or banana leaves

Preparation:
Soak cracked corn in water 8 to 12 hours, or overnight.

The next day, boil and drain corn. Grind it in a corn grinder (or a food processor) to make dough.

In a separate skillet, brown pork and chicken; remove and put aside.

In a different skillet (about 8 inches), prepare annatto oil (see tips under "All-In-One" recipe).

In a blender or a food processor, blend onion, garlic, culantro, peppers, and salt to create a sauce. (Divide sauce ½ and ½ and pour into two separate pots; one for the pork cubes and one for the chicken pieces). Add annatto oil to pork and chicken, making sure meat gets the red color of the annatto oil. Cook meat with sauce on low heat for a few minutes. Add 2 cups of water to each pot and let cook until tender.

Separate corn dough in ½: one for pork tamales and one for chicken tamales. Take sauce from the pot where the chicken was cooked and ladle sauce over dough to be used for chicken tamales. Pour enough sauce to add flavor and color to the dough. Taste dough, add more salt to dough if needed and keep kneading the dough. IMPORTANT: The process is the same for pork or chicken tamales.

Clean and cut *faldo* or banana leaves (see tips). Spread the leaves and place one large cooking spoon of corn dough onto the middle of the leaf. Then make a ball of the dough and flatten it. Pour 2 tablespoons of sauce over flattened dough for chicken tamales. On top place 2-3 pieces of meat, 2 olives, 1 prune and/or a few raisins.

Wrap tamales with leaves and tie them up with cooking thread so they stay wrapped. Cut thread into two-yard long lengths. Double bind all four sides of tamales with thread. The newly wrapped tamales are rectangular in shape (size 6 x 3 inches).

Fill a 24-quart stock pot ½ full of water, bring it to a boil and place as many tamales as you can fit in the pot. All tamales should be boiled for about 1 hour at a constant simmer. Remove and drain.

Serve warm and enjoy!

TIPS: Washing the leaves with warm water and leaving them out in the sun for 3-4 hours will make them softer and easier to work with. Use 14" pieces of leaves to wrap tamales. Faldo leaves are preferred because they give Panamanian tamales a very unique flavor. Use cooking thread to wrap tamales.

If banana leaves are used instead, dip them in warm water and let them dry to soften or just pass them over light flame to soften.

Wrapped Fresh Corn Tamales
(Tamales de maíz nuevo)

Serves 15 to 20

Ingredients:

6 cups fresh yellow corn kernels (or 30-40 ears of corn)

½ cup pork fat

1 cup chopped onion

2 chopped green bell peppers

6 chopped garlic cloves

1 finely chopped habanero pepper

2 tablespoons salt

2 cups water

Preparation:

Mix corn with water and pass through a coarse sieve thoroughly so that only the skin of the corn remains in the sieve. The batter should be thick.

Fry onion, garlic, and peppers in pork fat.

Add salt and habanero pepper and mix well. Add this to corn batter and mix well with a spoon.

Place the batter in one corn husk, cover with another and tie them up with a one-yard long string or cooking thread.

Fill a 24-quart pot ½ full of water, bring to a full rolling boil and place as many tamales as you can fit in the pot. All tamales should be boiled for about 1 hour at a constant simmer. Remove and drain.

Serve warm and enjoy!

CULTURAL NOTE: *Panamanian wrapped corn tamales are considered a national dish. Tamales are made, usually in large quantities, for special occasions: weddings, anniversaries, birthdays, and holidays, especially Christmas and New Year's Eve. People make them at home or can special order them. In Panama, there are basically three ways of making tamales: wrapped tamales (made with whole mature corn and cracked corn), wrapped fresh corn tamales, and tamale casserole (see the next recipe). The two recipes for wrapped tamales (above) are the original recipes of Ofelina Lasso (Nilsa's mother). Traditionally, in the rural areas, wrapped tamales are cooked out in the open over a fogón (a cooking area or rustic stove, usually constructed of bricks or stones).*

NOTE: *Reserve fresh corn husks. See tips on how to cut corn kernels from cob under "Corn Fritters" recipe.*

Tamale Casserole
(Tamal de olla)

Serves 8 to 10

Ingredients:

3 pounds corn dough

1 large red bell pepper (optional)

1 cup warm water

¼ cup annatto oil

Ingredients for sauce and stew:

2 pounds lean pork

½ cup oil

5 chopped medium red tomatoes

1 can (15 ounces) tomato sauce

1 finely chopped medium onion

5 minced garlic cloves

½ cup chopped green bell peppers

1 teaspoon All-purpose Adobo

½ cup chopped red bell peppers

3 cups water

½ chopped habanero pepper

¼ cup red wine

Julienned red peppers (optional)

1 teaspoon salt

Preparation:

Pour annatto oil and warm water on dough and knead until dough is firm. Set aside.

In a separate pot, prepare stew. Cut pork into small cubes and season with All-purpose Adobo. Add 3 cups of water and cook pork in pot until tender.

Blend onion, peppers, tomatoes, and garlic. Mix blended ingredients with tomato sauce and add them to pork.

Cook pork with all ingredients on low heat for approximately 10 minutes.

Add dough and stir with wooden spoon for 5 minutes. Cook on low heat 30 to 35 minutes. If necessary add more water until mixture is creamy or buttery.

Let stand for a few minutes and decorate top with red pepper strips (optional).

Serve warm.

NOTE: Homemade dough is preferred. See tips under "Corn Tortilla" recipe.

Corn Tortilla
(Tortilla panameña)

Serves 4 to 6

Ingredients:

2 pounds yellow corn dough

2 teaspoons corn or canola oil

3 cups water

Salt to taste

Preparation:

Knead dough, sprinkle salt and water, while kneading dough. Add water until dough is firm. Make a big ball with corn dough and flatten it to make a 9 or 10-inch around and over ½-inch thick tortilla.

Heat the *cazuela* on low heat. Pour and spread two tablespoons of oil in the *cazuela*. Put tortilla on the *cazuela* and cook until done inside and until both sides are crunchy and golden browned. Cover with faldo leaves or banana leaves, if available.

Serve hot with fresh white pressed cheese and coffee or tea. Traditionally, corn tortillas are cut into 4 or 6 pizza-like slices. Each slice is cut with a knife on the sides, making pockets. Place small pieces of white pressed cheese inside pockets.

TIPS: *Some supermarkets sell frozen corn dough but homemade is preferred. To make it at home, buy cracked corn, cook it and grind it (in a corn grinder or a food processor). Pour ½ cup of water to make dough firm. Add more water if necessary.*

Fresh Corn Tortilla

(Changa)

Serves 4 to 6

Ingredients:

3 cups fresh yellow corn kernels

1 cup All-purpose flour

3 teaspoons vegetable or corn oil or unsalted butter

1 teaspoon baking powder

2 tablespoons sugar (optional)

2 tablespoons oil or unsalted butter

Preparation:
Grind cut fresh corn in a corn grinder (or use a food processor) to create mix. Drain excess liquid to create soft dough.

Add flour, baking powder and sugar. Work dough for about 5 minutes. Add more flour to thicken dough, if necessary. Place dough in a *cazuela* or in a 10-inch cast iron skillet and flatten it to make a 9 or 10-inch round and over half-inch thick tortilla.

Heat the *cazuela* on low, spread oil or unsalted butter. Put tortilla on the *cazuela* and cover with faldo leaves or banana leaves, if available. Cook until both sides are crunchy or until lightly golden browned.

NOTE: If cast iron is used, grease with oil or butter. Place tortilla in the skillet, cover with aluminum foil and bake in a preheated 350°F oven 25 to 30 minutes, or until done.

Serve with fresh white pressed cheese and coffee. Traditionally, it is cut into 4 or 6 pizza-like slices. Each slice is cut with a knife on the sides to make a pocket. Place small pieces of white pressed cheese in pocket and enjoy.

Deep-Fried Corn Tortilla

(Tortilla frita)

Serves 4 to 6

Ingredients:

2 cups yellow corn meal

1 cup water

½ teaspoon sea salt

1 tablespoon canola oil

¼ teaspoon baking powder

Preparation:

Using wet hands and a wooden spoon, mix together all ingredients to make dough. Dough should be firm. Once dough is well-mixed, form into discs ¼-inch thick and about 3 inches in diameter.

Heat oil and deep-fry tortillas on medium heat. Fry them for 3 minutes, or until lightly browned.

Serve hot for breakfast with fresh white pressed cheese, sausages, eggs, orange juice, and coffee or tea.

CULTURAL NOTE: Did you know? The thickest corn tortilla in the world is made in Panama. Panamanian corn tortillas are different from those made in other parts of Latin America. The Webster's New International Dictionary defines the word "tortilla" as "a thin flat unleavened cake, as of maize, baked on a heated iron or stone." The word "tortilla" comes from the Spanish word "torta" which means "small cake" or "round cake." In Spanish, it denotes different types of foods: tortilla (as an omelet-like egg-based dish), Spanish-style or tortilla de patatas (an omelet-like tortilla, typically made with beaten eggs, pieces of potato, other ingredients and seasonings), and a flat thin cake of maize or flour which are popular in Mexico and in other parts of Latin America. The Panamanian changa and tortilla redefine the word "tortilla," since they are neither thin nor small. They definitely have much more flavor than other Latin American tortillas. Both changa and tortilla are large and thick corn cakes about 9 to 10 inches around and almost 1 inch thick. They are similar in size but the ways of preparation differ a bit. Changa is made of fresh yellow corn kernels and unsalted water, while corn tortilla is made with yellow mature corn, water and salt. Another Panamanian-style tortilla is the small and thick deep-fried corn tortilla similar to a deep-fried corn meal disc. All Panamanian-style corn tortillas are usually served as a main dish at breakfast and dinner, especially in rural Panama. Traditionally, Panama's thick tortillas and changas are cooked on a cazuela over a fogón. A Panamanian cazuela is a traditional flat cookware made of clay. A fogón is a cooking area or rustic stove, usually constructed of bricks or stones. It is commonly located across one corner of an opened country kitchen or out in the backyard.

TIPS: *Homemade corn dough is preferred. See tips under "Corn Tortilla" recipe.*

Corn Fritters
(Pastelitos de maíz)

Serves 10 to 12

Ingredients:

3 cups fresh yellow corn kernels

2 cups corn flour

1 teaspoon baking powder

1 can (15 ounces) cream style sweet corn

1 pinch sugar (optional)

Preparation:

Use corn grinder or food processor to grind corn.

Mix all ingredients to make a creamy mix.

Thicken mix with 2 cups of flour, use more if necessary.

Deep-fry, placing one tablespoon in hot oil. Cook until golden browned.

Serve warm for breakfast.

TIPS: To remove corn kernels from the cob use a large mixing bowl, stand the shucked corn cob upright, with the tip of cob placed in the center of the bowl. Hold the cob steady, use a sharp knife and make long downward strokes on the cob, separating the kernels from the cob.

Bollos

(Bollos de maíz viejo)

(mature corn dough wrapped in Royal Palm tree leaves)

Serves 12 to 14

Ingredients:

2-3 pounds mature yellow corn kernels

26 Royal Palm tree leaves

Cooking string

Salt to taste (optional)

Preparation:

Cook corn kernels for about 1 hour, or until soft. Save water where corn was boiled to prepare a traditional corn beverage (**see cultural note**).

Grind corn in a corn grinder or a food processor. Work dough for 5 minutes; add salt if desired.

Make softball-sized balls with dough. Give each ball a cylindrical shape.

Cut cooking thread into one-yard long lengths. Wash leaves and wrap each *bollo* with 2 leaves and tie it up with a piece of thread.

Boil newly wrapped *bollos* for about 40 minutes.

Drain and serve warm.

CULTURAL NOTE: This regular **bollo or bollo de maíz viejo** recipe is common across the nation. It is a traditional recipe, especially during the annual folkloric activity called "La Bollada, which takes place in the countryside. These bollos are usually served wrapped for breakfast. They can also be served as a side dish for lunch or dinner. Customarily, Panamanians recycle the water where the corn was boiled. They prepare a refreshing corn beverage or "agua de maíz" by adding sugar to taste. Everyone enjoys this drink which goes very well together with the freshly made bollos.

Stuffed Bollos
(Bollos preñados)

(fresh corn dough wrapped in corn husks or sugar cane leaves)

Serves 10 to 12

Ingredients:

4 pounds fresh yellow corn kernels

1 pound lean pork

¼ pound pork chorizo

1 large tomato

1 large onion

2 garlic cloves

6 large culantro leaves

4 large green peppers

Salt, hot sauce, and black pepper to taste

4 tablespoons tomato paste

1 can (8 ounces) tomato sauce

2 tablespoons canola oil

Sugar cane leaves or corn husks

Note: you will need cooking string

Preparation:

Blend tomato, onion, garlic, culantro, green pepper, oil, tomato sauce and paste, salt, black pepper, and hot sauce.

Cut pork and chorizo into small pieces; add mixed ingredients. Cook until done but don't let dry.

Wash leaves and place some dough in the center of the leaves (enough dough to make a 6-inch long and 2-inch thick *bollo*).

Put pork and pork sauce in the middle of the dough and cover it with more dough. Wrap it with leaves and tie it up with cooking string.

Boil newly wrapped *bollos* for about 40 minutes. Drain and serve warm.

TIPS: To make homemade dough, buy 30-45 fresh corn on the cob. See tips on how to cut corn kernels from cob under "Corn Fritters" recipe. Grind on a corn grinder or a food processor. Mix corn with water and pass through a coarse sieve thoroughly so that only the skin of the corn remains in the sieve. Dough should be soft but not watery.

VARIATION: Add coconut milk to make sweetened bollos with coconut milk. See tips under "Rice with Coconut" recipe.

Bollos de Chicharrón

(Corn meal dough wrapped in Royal Palm tree leaves)

Serves 50

Ingredients:

5 pounds cracked corn

2 pounds uncooked pork rinds/pork skin

2-3 cups water

Preparation:

Wash and cook corn for about 2 hours, or until soft. Grind it in a corn grinder or a food processor. Add water to make dough. Dough should have a soft consistency.

While kneading dough, pour some of the renderings of the fried pork and mix well with hands.

Use about 50 long Royal Palm tree leaves. With hands, place small amounts of dough in leaves, shaping it into a 6-inch long and 2-inch thick *bollo*. Wrap it with leaves and tie it up with a string, long enough to secure newly made *bollo*. Repeat process to make each *bollo*.

Boil *bollos* for about 40 minutes. Royal Palm tree leaves will give *bollos* a very traditional and unique flavor.

Drain and serve hot or warm.

CULTURAL NOTE: *Southwest of Panama City one finds La Chorrera, one of the largest cities in the country. It is famous for its international fair and for its **bollos de maíz preñado** (fresh corn dough filled with pork and pork chorizo wrapped in sugar cane leaves and boiled), and **bollos de chicharrón** (in the process of making the fried pork rinds, the renderings of the pork are mixed in with the corn dough and later wrapped in Royal Palm tree leaves and boiled). Bollo de chicharrón is a dish brought to Panama by Afro-Antilleans. **Bollos chorreranos** (bollos from La Chorrera) are very filling and can be served as a main dish, side dish or snack. They are popular, delicious and economical. These bollos sell for less than 1.00 USD each.*

Bollos Changos

(Thick sweetened corn meal paste wrapped in corn husk)

Serves 16 to 20

Ingredients:

25 fresh corn on the cob (save corn husks)

3-4 cups instant corn dough mix

2 teaspoons salt

½ cup sugar

1 cup coconut milk (optional)

Preparation:

Select fresh corn on the cob with a good husk. Cut the base of the corn cob to remove the husk without destroying it. Cut the base and twist corn to remove it. Remove corn kernels from the cob with a sharp knife and grind corn in a grinder or a food processor (see tips under "Corn Fritters" recipe).

In a large bowl, bring together corn paste, instant corn dough mix, salt, sugar, and coconut milk. Mix well with a wooden spoon and set aside.

Cut cooking thread into one-yard long lengths to tie up the ends of the corn husks. Fill husks with two to three spoonfuls of the mixture. Tie up around wrapping to keep mixture inside husk. The newly wrapped *bollo* must give the appearance of fresh corn.

Fill a 12-quart pot ½ full of water, bring to a full rolling boil and place as many *bollos* as you can fit in the pot. All *bollos* should be boiled for about 1 hour at a constant simmer. Remove and drain.

Serve them warm with white cheese and/or butter slices.

Chiricano-Style Bollos
(Bollos chiricanos)

(sweetened corn dough wrapped in plantain leaves)

Serves 10 to 12

Ingredients:

2 cups corn dough

¾ crushed panela

1 teaspoon anise seeds

1 tablespoon margarine or butter

Note: you will need 5-6 plantain leaves

Preparation:

Add all ingredients to corn dough, kneading well.

Make 3 to 3 ½ -inch long rolls (stretch until they look thin and elongated) and wrap them in plantain leaves.

Bake in oven at 350°F for about 45 minutes.

Bollo de Cuajá or Cuajada
(from Chiriqui)

Serves 16 to 20

Ingredients:

2 pounds corn dough

1 ½ cups milk

¼ pound butter or margarine

1 pound white cheese

Salt to taste

Note: you will need 8-10 plantain leaves

Preparation:

Add all ingredients to corn dough (milk last), kneading well.

Make 4-inch long rolls (stretch until they look thin and elongated) and wrap them in plantain leaves.

Bake in oven at 350ºF for about 45 minutes.

TIPS: Homemade corn dough is preferred. See tips under "Corn Tortilla" recipe.

Serén or Mandungo Salado

Serves 8 to 10

Ingredients:

25 fresh corn on the cob

3 pounds salted ham hock

8 chopped culantro leaves

1 pound chopped yellow pear tomatoes

3 tablespoons annatto oil

8 sweet peppers

1 chopped large onion

½ teaspoon oregano

Pepper and salt to taste

4-5 cups water

Preparation:

Brown ham hock; add culantro, tomatoes, sweet peppers, oregano, annatto oil, and onion.

Add 4 to 5 cups of water and cook on low until ham hock is done, but don't let dry. Set aside.

Cut corn kernels from cob (see tips under "Corn Fritters" recipe). Grind corn in a corn grinder or a food processor.

Strain and use only corn juice; add 1 cup of water.

Season to taste with salt and pepper and cook on medium-low for about 1 hour. Stir constantly! When thickens, turn heat down; add ham hock and sauce. Keep mixing with a wooden spoon 20 to 25 minutes.

Serve warm in bowls and enjoy!

CUTURAL NOTE: Serén is a thick corn soup-like dish. In Panama, there are variations of it: salted white serén, sweetened serén, and serén Zambo. The main ingredients in salted serén are fresh corn and salted ham hock (shown above). Sweetened serén is also a soup-like dish, but instead of adding salted ingredients, Panamanians enhance it with cane syrup or panela and serve it with white cheese on top. Serén Zambo is also sweet, but it's prepared with lightly fermented corn juice. These dishes are very popular in the central provinces, especially in Chitre, the capital of the province of Herrera.

Almojábanos

Serves (varies)

Ingredients:

2 pounds cracked corn

1 ½ pounds grated or melted fresh white cheese

1 tablespoon sugar

1 ½ teaspoons kosher salt

3 tablespoons softened unsalted butter

1 ½ teaspoons baking powder

Preparation:

To make dough, boil and grind corn in a corn grinder or a food processor; add sugar, salt, cheese, and butter. Knead dough until smooth.

Pull off pieces of dough and roll into balls 1½ -inch in diameter.

Deep-fry in hot oil until lightly golden.

CULTURAL NOTE: Almojábanas or almojábanos is typical of some South American countries and the Caribbean. In Colombia, for example, they are known as almojábanas or Colombian cheese rolls. They are made with masarepa corn meal, cheese, and eggs. In Colombia almojábanas are baked and made with a soft farmer's cheese called cuajada or a combination of ricotta and farmer's cheese. In Puerto Rico, almojábanas (or a rice meal cruller) are made with flour, rice meal, and grated native cheese. It is deep-fried. In Panama, almojábanos are made with homemade corn dough and grated or melted fresh white cheese (like Queso Fresco). They are always deep-fried. Almojábanos are very popular in the province of Chiriqui, where they stand out for their unique shape, more like an elongated "S" shape. In Chiriqui, people seem to prefer fresh yellow corn kernels, instead of cracked corn (the recipe above is a variation). This dish is served hot or warm for breakfast or as a mid-morning snack with coffee. They can also be served as a side dish with the Panamanian tasajo (smoked and cured beef).

Hot Corn Cereal

Serves 4

Ingredients:

1 cup corn meal

1 cup milk

1 cup water

Brown sugar to taste

Vanilla to taste

Nutmeg to taste

Preparation:

Pour milk and water in saucepan and whisk in corn meal. Turn the flame on to medium and bring to a boil, stirring sporadically.

Simmer on low heat for a few minutes, or until cereal is thickened; add brown sugar, nutmeg, and vanilla and mix.

Serve warm.

Traditional Creamed Corn

Serves 4

Ingredients:

3-4 cups of fresh corn kernels (about 3+ ears)

¾ cup low-fat or whole milk

1 tablespoon cornstarch

1 teaspoon salt.

Preparation:

Place about 3 cups of corn, milk, and cornstarch in a blender; blend until smooth. Reserve one cup of corn for later.

Pour puree into a saucepan; add in reserved corn to the saucepan.

Cook over high-medium heat 5 to 8 minutes, or until mixture thickens and corn becomes tender.

Serve hot or warm as breakfast or as a side dish.

Alfajores

Serves 10-12

Ingredients:

1 pound dry corn

1 cup cane syrup

½ cup finely minced ginger root

Preparation:

Toast corn in a heavy bottomed pan over a medium heat, until golden. Do not let pop.

Grind corn and return it to the pan; add cane syrup and ginger. Cook, stirring consistently, until the mixture begins to separate from the bottom of the pan. Divide into small pieces while still warm.

Serve with bland, soft or pressed white cheese over fresh orange leaves.

Cou Cou

Serves 4

Ingredients:

2 cups yellow corn meal

1 Package frozen cut okra

6 cups water

¼ cup butter

Salt to taste

Preparation:

In a large saucepan, bring three of the six cups of water to a boil.

Add okra and boil for two minutes.

Mix the rest of water with corn meal and add it to okra.

Cook and stir corn meal and okra until the corn meal is soft and thick.

Add butter and salt to taste and serve hot.

CULTURAL NOTE: This recipe is based on the original recipe from Barbados and Jamaica. It is a staple food of Afro-Panamanians in Panama City, Colon, and Bocas del Toro.

TIPS: Take the leftover cou cou and put it in a square loft pan, refrigerate, slice and pan-fry. Serve as a snack or side dish.

PASTA
AND
NOODLES

P asta, a traditional Italian food, has definitely become an international staple. Demetri, in his article "Italian Pasta Through the Ages," reports that "there is some evidence of an Etrusco-Roman noodle [in the Etruria region – today the central western portion of Italy] made from the same durum wheat as modern pasta called *lagane* (origin of the modern word for lasagna). However this food, first mentioned in the 1st century AD was not boiled like pasta, it was cooked in an oven. Therefore ancient *lagane* had some similarities, but cannot be considered pasta." Regarding the origin of dried pasta, he adds: "Like so much of southern Italian life, the Arab invasions of the 8th century heavily influenced the regional cuisine and is the most accepted theory for the introduction of pasta. The dried noodle-like product they introduced to Sicily is most likely the origins of dried pasta...There are roughly 350 different shapes and varieties of dried pasta in Italy, even more counting regional differences." Chefs on *Cheftalk.com* discuss the origin of Chinese noodles. They point out that "around the 3rd century BC, when the Roman Empire began trading with the Chinese Han Empire in China, merchants and nomads carried the grindstone from oasis to oasis along the Silk Roads. For the first time, the Chinese began grinding wheat into flour instead of cooking it whole...They made noodles, dumplings, thin pancakes, stuffed buns, and steamed breads." In Panama, pasta and noodles are a direct influence of European and Chinese cuisine. The most familiar dried pasta is spaghetti. Most Panamanians enjoy spaghetti and chicken as a special Sunday dinner. Panamanians also love Chinese noodles in a variety of ways.

Spaghetti with Chicken
(Macarrones con gallina)

Serves 6 to 8

Ingredients:

1 whole chicken cut in pieces (3 pounds)

1 pound of spaghetti

6 minced garlic cloves

1 can (29 ounces) diced tomatoes

1 chopped large onion

2 cups chicken stock

2 (8 ounces) can tomato sauce

½ teaspoon sugar

2 dried basil leaves

2 laurel leaves

Salt, pepper and oregano to taste

2 tablespoons olive oil

Parmesan cheese

Preparation:
Season chicken pieces with salt, pepper, 3 garlic cloves, and oregano.

Heat oil in a 4-quart pot, cook and stir onion and garlic.

Add chicken and cook on low for 10 minutes; add diced tomato and cook for few minutes.

Add chicken stock, tomato sauce, and sugar; cook at medium heat until chicken is tender.

Meanwhile, fill an 8-quart pot with water, bring to a full rolling boil and add oregano, laurel and basil leaves, salt, and spaghetti; cook until spaghetti is al dente.

Drain spaghetti, mix with chicken sauce, serve and sprinkle with parmesan cheese.

Johny Mazzetti

Serves 6 to 8

Ingredients:

1 pound pack cooked noodles or elbow macaroni

1 ½ pounds ground beef

1 large chopped onion

1 medium red bell pepper

1 can (8 ounces) tomato sauce (or mushroom soup)

1 can (29 ounces) chopped tomato

1 can (6 ounces) mushrooms

1 jar (6 ounces) chopped stuffed olives

½ pound grated American cheese

¼ pound grated mozzarella cheese

¼ pound grated cheddar cheese

1 chopped celery stalk

2 tablespoons canola oil

4 cooked and crumbled bacon strips

1 minced garlic clove

Preparation:

Heat oil in a large skillet, cook and stir onion until transparent, add garlic, bell pepper, and celery.

Cook and stir ingredients for 5 minutes, remove from the skillet and add ground beef.

After browning ground beef, add mushrooms, onion mix, chopped tomatoes, tomato sauce, and olives; mix and cook together for 5 minutes.

Add mix and cheeses to noodles. Reserve ½ of American cheese for the topping.

Pour noodle mix into a large casserole, sprinkle with bacon and remaining cheese on top.

Bake at 425°F for 20 minutes, or until cheese is lightly browned.

CULTURAL NOTE: *We made some modifications of our own to this Panama Canal-party favorite. We added and omitted some ingredients to represent the way the home cook could put his/her own personal touch.*

TIPS: the ground beef can be substituted with ground turkey.

Bacon can be omitted.

Chicken Chow Mein

Serves 8

Ingredients:

2 cups boneless skinless chicken breasts (cooked and cut into bite-size pieces)

10 ounces dried medium Chinese noodles

3 sliced fresh celery stalks

1 diced or shredded carrot

3 sliced cabbage leaves

4 chopped scallions

1-2 cups trimmed snow peas or Chinese bean sprouts

2 tablespoons olive oil or canola oil

3 tablespoons cornstarch

1 can (10 ounces) condensed chicken broth

¼ cup soy sauce

¼ cup water

Preparation:

Heat oil in a large pot; cook and stir celery until crisp-tender.

Add chicken and remaining vegetables.

In a bowl, mix cornstarch with water until smooth and add chicken broth and soy sauce.

Mix well and pour over chicken and vegetables.

Cook and stir until sauce thickens. Reduce heat to low and cover and simmer 10 to 15 minutes.

Mix with hot cooked noodles and serve.

CULTURAL NOTE: *This is the original recipe of Xenia Gutiérrez (Nilsa's oldest sister). Panamanian families usually serve this dish at Sunday dinners or birthdays. It is a very common dish at Chinese restaurants across the nation.*

Lo Hon Chai

Serves 6 to 8

Ingredients:

1 (6 ounces) package rehydrated cellophane/glass noodles

1 cup black fungus

10 halved/rehydrated shitake mushrooms

1 sliced medium carrot

1 (12 ounces) cubed firm tofu

1 cup snap peas

10 chopped Chinese cabbage leaves

8 halved broccoli florets

1 sliced medium zucchini

3 sliced large celery stalks

1 cup sliced ginger root

2 tablespoons canola oil

3 minced garlic cloves

Ingredients for Seasoning:

2 cubes preserved bean curd

3 tablespoons soy sauce

3 tablespoons shitake mushroom sauce or vegetarian soy sauce

1 tablespoon sesame oil

3 tablespoons Chinese cooking wine

1 tablespoon sugar

1 teaspoon salt

pepper to taste

½ cup vegetable broth

Preparation:

Heat oil in a large pot over medium low; cook garlic and ginger until fragrant, add shitake mushrooms.

Season to taste with salt and pepper.

Add black fungus and simmer on low 2 to 3 minutes.

Add carrots and Chinese cabbage and cook until cabbage wilts a little.

Add ingredients for seasonings, except the broth. Mix well and cook for 5 minutes.

In a separate skillet, pan fry tofu cubes. Set aside.

Add broth, tofu, celery, zucchini, and snap peas; cook until it bubbles.

Add noodles and broccoli at the very end and let cook for 2 minutes and serve.

PLANTAINS

AND

BANANAS

Although bananas and plantains are members of the same family, they are different. They are used as a vegetable in many recipes, especially in Africa, the Caribbean, and Latin America. Plantains have definitely become more popular and widely available in the U.S. They can be found in the fresh produce section of supermarkets, some farmers' markets and markets that carry Latin produce. Plantains must be cooked before serving. They are highly nutritious: good source of potassium and vitamins A and C, high in fiber and in carbohydrates. They have a thicker skin and are usually longer than bananas. They are green when not fully ripe, and yellow or black when very ripe. On the contrary, bananas are creamier than plantains and are eaten as fruit when sweet and yellow. They are green when not fully ripe and yellow when ripe. Like plantains, bananas contain vitamin C, potassium and dietary fiber. They are also an energy booster because they contain natural sugars.

Panama is a minor producer of plantain and Panamanians can't have enough of it. Ripe and green plantains are definitely very popular across the nation, as they are the main ingredient in many recipes. They can be fried, boiled, sun-dried and baked. They can be used to make various dishes: soups, desserts, cereals, chips, pureed foods, empanadas, pancakes, *bollos*, and many others. Bananas are popular in shakes, and can be eaten mashed and fried, for example: mashed banana or banana *chocao*, banana fritters and *Ngöbe- Buglé*-style banana balls. Bananas and plantains are sold in supermarkets, farmers' markets and street stands.

Twice-Fried Plantains

(Patacones)

Serves 4

Ingredients:

2 large green plantains

2 cups canola oil

Salt to taste

Preparation:

Heat oil in a medium skillet on low before peeling plantains. When done peeling, increase flame to medium-high.

Peel plantains (see tips), slice into ½ -inch-thick rounds, sprinkle salt and fry in hot oil immediately. Carefully, slip plantain pieces into oil. Fry until fork tender, or until golden.

Remove and place plantain rounds on paper towels; lower heat.

Place plantain rounds on cutting board and carefully flatten each round with a kitchen mallet or a *tostonera* (see note); sprinkle salt to taste and fry again.

Reheat oil or increase heat to medium-high. When oil is hot, fry flattened round pieces, turning once until golden brown.

Drain on paper towels and sprinkle more salt.

Serve while hot and crunchy.

NOTE: A tostonera is used to mash plantain rounds. This little device is made of two pieces of wood with handles on one end. The two pieces are connected with a hinge on the opposite end. Flatten pieces of plantain by placing them between the two pieces of wood and pressing the handles together.

TIPS: How to peel plantains? Cut off 1inch at both ends. With a paring knife, cut along plantain, making a slit through the peel down to (but not into) the flesh. Starting at one end, peel back the skin. Try to use them right after peeling, otherwise they will turn dark. To keep them from turning dark, soak them in a bowl of cold water.

Plantain Chips

(Platanitos)

Serves 6 to 8

Ingredients:

3 peeled green plantains

Salt to taste

Garlic powder to taste (optional)

Canola oil (for frying)

Preparation:

Preheat oil in a deep sided skillet or deep-fryer on medium-high heat to 360°F.

Using a mandolin or sharp knife, slice plantains into 1/8-inch thick ovals on the diagonal. Place slices in cool water for 30 minutes. Drain and dry.

Carefully add plantains to the oil in batches and fry for about 1 minute, or until crispy.

Remove and place over paper towel-lined plate; sprinkle lightly with garlic, and salt.

Transfer to a serving plate and serve.

Plantains in Temptation

(Plátanos en tentación)

Serves 4 to 6

Ingredients:

2 ripe plantains

1 ½ cups water

1 ½ cups pure cane dark brown sugar

1 cinnamon stick

1 tablespoon ground cinnamon (to decorate)

Preparation:

Peel and cut plantains in small round pieces (about 3-inch long)

Put water, plantain pieces, and cinnamon stick in a pan and cook at medium-high heat. Wait until it boils.

Add sugar while stirring. Simmer for a few minutes over low heat. The natural sugars of plantains will caramelize with brown sugar. At this stage they are ready.

Serve and garnish with ground cinnamon.

CULTURAL NOTE: Plantains in temptation are one of the most popular plantain based side dishes in Panama. They are absolutely delicious with almost any type of rice: white, rice with green pigeon peas and coconut, Panamanian-Style rice with chicken, etc. (see RICE section for more rice recipes).

Plantain Chocao

(Chocao de plátano)

Serves 4 to 6
Ingredients:
4 ripe plantains
½ cup milk
6 cups water
3 cinnamon sticks (optional)
Dash cinnamon powder (optional)

Preparation:
Pour water in a large pot and bring to a full rolling boil.

Cut off 1 or 1 ½ inches at both ends of plantains. Cut unpeeled plantains into 3-inch rounds. Place pieces and 3 cinnamon sticks in boiling water. Cook for 25 minutes, or until soft. Let stand 5 to 10 minutes, then drain water, peel plantain pieces and place them in a mixing bowl.

Carefully, mash plantains with a potato masher. Add ½ cup of milk and mix with a wooden spoon.
Sprinkle cinnamon powder on top and serve.

NOTE: Cinnamon sticks can be reused to decorate the plate.

VARIATION: to make mashed ripe banana (chocao), peel ripe bananas, mash them, add milk, and mix well. Sprinkle with cinnamon powder. Cinnamon sticks are just for decoration.

Chocao

(A variation of previous recipe)

Serves 6 to 8

Ingredients:

8 very ripe plantains

3 cups grated fresh coconut

¼ cup grated ginger

1 teaspoon salt

Sugar to taste

Preparation:

Peel and cut plantains in rounds. In a medium pan, boil until soft and drain.

Extract coconut milk from grated coconut (see tips under "Rice with Coconut" recipe); add coconut milk and ginger to boiled plantains. Cook for 15 minutes.

Add sugar and salt. Let cook 5 to 8 additional minutes.

Baked Plantain
(Plátano asado)

Serves 4

Ingredients:

2 green or ripe plantains

Preparation:

Green plantains: Peel plantain; bake in oven at 350°F 1 hour, or until tender. Serve hot.

Ripe plantains: Cut ends of ripe plantain; bake in oven at 350°F about 1 hour. It is done when peeling bursts.

Remove peeling, butter and place in oven 5 to 8 additional minutes.

Tajadas

Serves 6 to 8

Ingredients:

3 very ripe plantains

Canola oil (for frying)

Preparation:

Peel plantains; cut in halves and slice lengthwise into 4 or 5 slices each.

Fry until tender and golden brown. Remove and place over paper towel-lined plate.

Serve with any recipe rice, as a side dish.

Muogo

Serves 6 to 8

Ingredients:

10 green bananas

2 grated coconuts

1 can (6 ounces) evaporated milk

4 tablespoons pure vanilla extract

1 teaspoon ground cinnamon

6 cloves

1 teaspoon nutmeg

Sugar to taste

Preparation:

Peel and boil bananas until soft; add cloves to boiling bananas.

Meanwhile, extract coconut milk from grated coconut (see tips under "Rice with Coconut recipe).

Remove cloves; mash bananas to make puree.

Add all ingredients to puree; cook on low for 5 minutes, stirring until creamy.

It's a delicious banana cream recipe!

Banana Fritters
(Frituras de guineo)

Serves 4 to 6

Ingredients:

4 ripe bananas

6 tablespoons sugar

½ teaspoon salt

1 ½ teaspoons baking powder

1 teaspoon cinnamon

1 cup flour

½ cup milk

½ teaspoon nutmeg

1 teaspoon vanilla

Preparation:

Mix flour, baking powder, salt, cinnamon, and nutmeg.

In separate bowl, mash bananas; add sugar, milk, and vanilla.

Add dry ingredients and mix well.

Divide into small balls. Flatten them and deep-fry at medium heat, until brown on both sides.

Drain them on paper towels and serve warm.

Banana Balls

(Bolas de guineo)

Serves 4 to 6

Ingredients:

4 ripe bananas

2 green bananas

½ cup powdered sugar

2 plantain leaves

Ground cinnamon to taste

Preparation:

Peel bananas; boil only green bananas until soft.

Mash bananas together with a wooden masher or a potato masher.

Make small banana balls, rolling them on powdered sugar; sprinkle cinnamon and serve over plantain leaves.

CULTURAL NOTE: This recipe is a variation of the banana balls made by the Ngöbe-Buglé tribes. The Ngöbe-Buglé is an indigenous territory located in the western Panamanian provinces of Bocas del Toro, Chiriqui, Cocle, and Veraguas. They are the largest indigenous group in Panama and have a high degree of administrative autonomy. The Ngöbe and the Buglé tribes are closely associated and collectively referred to as the Guaymí people, even though they are two separate groups of people.

Banana Tarte with Callaloo

(Torta de banano con Kalalú)

Serves 8 to 10

Ingredients:

2 pounds green bananas

2 eggs

5 callaloo leaves

1 sweet pepper

Salt and pepper to taste

Vegetable oil (for frying)

Preparation:

Cook callaloo leaves until soft.

Grate green bananas.

Chop all vegetables; add grated banana, eggs, salt, and pepper to taste. Mix well.

Fry mixture, placing one tablespoon in hot oil; cook 5 to 8 minutes, or until done.

Serve warm.

Mamita

Serves 4

Ingredients:

20 green bananas

1 coconut or 1 can of coconut cream

Dash salt

Preparation:

Peel and boil green bananas with salt. After they are cooked mash banana and mix in the coconut cream.

CULTURAL NOTE: This dish is usually served with fish in the area of Portobelo, province of Colon, where the Afro-Panamanians represent the majority of the population.

Goyoría

Serves 6 to 8

Ingredients:

3 green plantains

2 cups cane syrup

Canola oil (for frying)

Preparation:

Peel plantains and cut into thin chips; fry in hot oil until golden.

Bring the syrup to a boil in a saucepan over medium heat and add fried plantain; stir constantly so it does not stick to the pan.

When syrup is thickened and starts to separate from the sides of the pan, remove and spoon mixture into small mounds on a serving dish lined with waxed paper.

CULTURAL NOTE: Golloría or goyoría means "exquisite dish." This definition fits the delicious Panamanian golloría. Traditionally, this dish is enjoyed as a dessert during Holy Week.

Chucula or Madun Kuna Yala

Serves 4 to 6

Ingredients:

2 very ripe plantains

1 coconut in chunks (save coconut water)

Preparation:

Boil plantains 10 to 15 minutes, or until cooked; remove from stove and place in mixing bowl. Sprinkle coconut water to taste, while mashing boiled plantains.

Serve with chunks of coconut.

CULTURAL NOTE: Chucula is a very traditional Kuna Yala dish. The indigenous Kuna or Cuna people can be found in the San Blas Islands, located just off the Caribbean coast of Panama, in the east part of the province of Panamá. They can also be found in the district of Chepo, province of Panama, and in the deep jungle of province of Darien.

Drunken Plantains

Serves 8 to 10

Ingredients:

6 ripe plantains

1½ cups sugar

½ cup lemon juice

4 teaspoons melted butter

½ cup rum

1 teaspoon ground cinnamon

Preparation:

Preheat oven to 350°F.

Peel plantains and cut in half lengthwise. Place plantains in a shallow baking dish, brush them all over with butter, rum, and lemon juice. Sprinkle sugar evenly.

Bake 25 to 30 minutes, or until soft. Note: Sugar will melt into rum and lemon juice to make syrup.

Sprinkle cinnamon and serve.

Plantain Bollo

Serves 4 to 6

Ingredients:

4 ripe plantains

2 green plantains

½ cup cane syrup

Grated ginger to taste

2 plantain leaves

Note: you will need cooking string

Preparation:

Boil green plantains. Grind green and ripe plantains in a grinder or a food processor; add cane syrup and ginger and mix well.

Cut plantain leaves into four sections. Place small amounts of mixture in each section of leaves, shaping it into a 6-inch long and 2-inch thick *bollo*. Wrap it with leaves and tie it up with a string.

Boil *bollos* about 40 minutes; drain and serve hot or warm.

Ripe Plantain with Cheese
(Plátano maduro con queso)

Serves 4

Ingredients:

3 ripe plantains

½ cup butter

White cheese to taste (like Queso Fresco)

Canola oil (for frying)

Preparation:

Peel plantains and cut in half lengthwise.

Wash plantains with salted water and brown in frying pan with butter.

Make a lengthwise slit in the middle of each piece of plantain; place a thin slice of cheese in the middle.

Deep-fry until golden. Serve warm as appetizer or as side dish.

Green Plantain Mazamorra
(Mazamorra de plátano verde)

Serves 4 to 6

Ingredients:

4 green plantains

1 can (12 ounces) condensed milk

1 tablespoon pure vanilla extract

1 tablespoon ground cinnamon

Ginger to taste

Preparation:

Peel and cook plantains; grind in a food processor and place in a large saucepan.

Add cinnamon, milk, vanilla, and ginger; cook 15 to 20 minutes.

Serve warm or cool.

CULTURAL NOTE: *This recipe is from the Community of Mamoní, Panama.*

Plantain Pancake
(Panqueque de plátano)

Serves 4

Ingredients:

1 ½ cups plantain dough

3 teaspoons baking powder

3 tablespoons sugar

1 tablespoon salt

3 eggs

1 ½ cups milk

3 tablespoons melted butter

Preparation:

Add baking powder, sugar, and salt to plantain dough.

Separate egg yolk from egg white; beat egg yolk until smooth. Add milk, mixing well.

Add mixture to plantain dough, beating consistently until soft.

Add melted butter and egg white. Mix well.

To make one pancake, place two serving spoons of mixture in a lightly greased skillet. Fry pancakes one at a time.

Serve with butter, honey or your favorite syrup.

TIPS: *To make plantain dough, peel 4-5 green plantains. Slice into 1 to 2-inch-thick rounds and grind in a food processor until mix is smooth.*

Plantain Fritters
(Pastelitos de plátano)

Serves 4

Ingredients:

2 cups mash ripe plantain

2 teaspoons butter

1 egg

5 tablespoons All-purpose flour

¼ cup milk

Salt to taste

Canola oil (for frying)

Preparation:

Mix plantain with butter, salt, milk, and flour.

Separate egg yolk from egg white; beat egg yolk. Add to mixture and blend well.

Fry one spoon at a time in hot canola oil or vegetable shortening; drain over paper towels.

Serve as a side dish.

Hot Plantain Cereal
(Crema de plátano)

Serves 4 to 6

Ingredients:

3-4 green plantains

3 cups water

1½ cups evaporated milk

1 tablespoon pure vanilla extract (optional)

Sugar to taste

Preparation:

Peel plantains and cut in half lengthwise.

Bake in oven at 350°F for 30 minutes, or until dry.

Grind in a food processor or a blender until it looks like wheat flour; add water and cook on low until thickened.

Add milk and sugar; simmer 10 to 15 additional minutes. Note: If it's too thick, add more water or milk.

Serve warm in a bowl.

CULTURAL NOTE: *This is the original recipe of Nilsa's mother, who got it from her mother. In El llano or Bayano, where she was born, people dry plantains out in the sun. It is the traditional method!*

Plantain Soup
(Sopa de plátano)

Serves 6 to 8

Ingredients:

1 pound stew beef

4 green plantains

10 cups water

1 tablespoon salt

4 minced garlic cloves

2 culantro leaves

1 cup chopped fresh parsley

1 chopped large onion

3 diced medium tomatoes

2 chopped green peppers

1 tablespoon canola oil or butter

Preparation:

Brown beef in a lightly greased skillet.

In a large pot, pour water and add beef; cover and cook over medium-high heat for 1 hour. Skim off fat from top.

Add all ingredients, except plantains. Cover and let cook until beef is tender.

Strain broth and pour into a separate pan. Set aside. Note: You will only need broth for this recipe. The meat can be used for another recipe, for example, "Shredded beef" or "Ropa vieja."

Peel plantains and cut into thin slices; brown them with oil or butter in a frying pan. Grind in a food processor or a blender until pulverized.

Add to soup and simmer 20 to 25 minutes.

Serve warm.

Plantain Pudding
(Pudín de plátano)

Serves 6

Ingredients:

3 cups cooked and mashed ripe plantains

½ cup sugar

6 tablespoons flour

1 teaspoon salt

1 teaspoon ground cinnamon

2 cups milk

½ cup butter

6 eggs

6 teaspoons sugar

Preparation:

Grease a soufflé dish and pre-heat the oven to 350°F.

In a pan combine ½ cup sugar, flour, salt, cinnamon, and milk. Mix well until lumps are dissolved. Stir over a fire until mixture thickens. Remove from heat.

Separate egg yolks from egg whites. Add egg yolks, butter, and plantain to mixture, stirring well after each addition. Bake in the oven for 25 minutes.

Whip egg whites until fluffy and slowly begin to add 6 teaspoons of sugar to make meringue.

Remove cake from the oven and cover it with meringue. Return to oven to lightly brown meringue.

TIPS: *Plantains should be yellow-ripe before cooking. Mash while they are still hot. Use a potato masher.*

Ripe Plantain Pie
(Pastel de plátano maduro)

Serves 8 to 10

Ingredients:

6 ripe plantains

4 tablespoons canola oil

2 chopped medium onions

6 chopped garlic cloves

2 chopped green peppers

1 can (8 ounces) tomato paste

2 teaspoons salt

½ teaspoon black pepper

2 finely chopped culantro leaves

½ cup red or white wine

1 cup water

2 chickens (3 pounds each)

Ingredients for topping:

5 eggs

5 tablespoons All-purpose flour

4 tablespoons sugar

½ teaspoon baking powder

Preparation:

Peel plantains and cut in half lengthwise pieces; fry in hot oil until golden brown on both sides.

Cover bottom of a large rectangular pyrex bakeware with plantains. Reserve some plantain pieces for later.

Heat oil in a large pot and fry onions, garlic, peppers, and culantro; add tomato paste and salt. Mix and add water and wine.

Cut chicken into pieces and add to the pot. Cook everything on low, until chicken is tender and sauce thickens. Remove chicken and let cool. Debone and take off skin.

Arrange chicken with sauce on top of plantain in the pyrex, then add a layer of plantains. Repeat the procedure until you are out of plantain, making sure the last layer is of plantains.

Preparation for topping:

Beat egg whites with an electric mixer on low speed until frothy and bubbly; add sugar slowly and mix to obtain a glossy and an evenly textured meringue.

Separately, whip egg yolks with flour and baking powder. Fold in egg yolks into the meringue and spread over the top of plantain layer.

Place pie in a 350°F oven 10 to 12 minutes, or until top is lightly browned.

Plantain Marmalade or Jam
(Mermelada de plátano)

Serves (varies)

Ingredients:

2 ripe plantains

1 cup sugar

¼ cup water

1 teaspoon lemon juice

Preparation:

Peel and mash plantains.   Pass through strainer; add lemon juice.

Cook over medium-low heat and add sugar; mix consistently until thickens.

It's ready when it looks transparent.

Let cool and serve with bread.

CULTURAL NOTE: *This recipe is from the community of Mamoní, Panama.*

Mogollo

Serves 4 to 6

Ingredients:

4 green plantains

4-5 tablespoons creamy peanut butter spread

½ pound pressed white cheese (Queso Fresco or Farmer's cheese)

4 cups water

Salt to taste

Preparation:

Pour water into a pot and add salt. Peel and boil plantains until soft.

Mash plantains; add peanut butter and mix well.

Make a long roll and cut into round pieces.

Place slices of cheese on top.

Serve for breakfast or as a side dish for dinner.

Plantain Dumplings
(Dumplings de plátano)

Serves 4 to 6

Ingredients:

4 green plantains

1 egg

1 pound All-purpose flour

1 cup fresh coconut milk

3-4 cups water

Salt to taste

Preparation:

Pour water into a pot and add salt. Peel and boil plantains until soft. Drain plantains and reserve water.

In a mixing bowl, mash plantains; slowly pour coconut milk, while mashing them. Add egg and mix well.

Add small portions of flour to the plantain mixture, until all flour is gone.

Make small balls and drop them into boiling reserved water. You can also drop balls into a boiling juicy stew or soup.

Cover and simmer for 15 minutes.

BEANS, LENTILS, AND OTHER LEGUMES

P anamanians eat a variety of beans and legumes. Beans are usually served with white rice at lunch and dinner. The most popular are red kidney beans. Lentils are commonly served as soups and stews. Other popular legumes are peas, lima beans, garbanzo or chickpeas. Beans, lentils, and other legumes are basic ingredients in some rice recipes, vegetarian dishes, and desserts. Most Panamanians prefer to use dried legumes.

Pork and Beans
(Puerco con frijoles)

Serves 8 to10

Ingredients:

½ pound pork boneless stew meat

½ pound dried black or red beans

2 cups chopped onion

1 cup chopped green onion

4 minced garlic cloves

½ cup culantro

1½ tablespoons salt

2 packs Goya annatto and culantro seasoning

3 cups of water

Preparation

Soak beans 6 to 8 hours. After soaking, rinse beans several times.

Pour water in a slow cooker; add pork, beans, and salt. Cover beans with three times their volume of water.

Cover and cook on high for 4 hours, or until done.

Add onion, culantro, garlic, salt, and seasoning.

Cover and cook on low for 35 minutes.

TIPS: *washing and soaking will release excess gas from the beans.*

Beans are done when they can be easily mashed between two fingers or with a fork.

Panamanian Lentil Soup
(Sopa de lentejas)

Serves 8 to10

Ingredients:

1 pound lentils

2 pounds stew beef

1 large onion

1 small chopped carrot

½ cup chopped parsley

3 chopped celery stalks (leaf only)

1 chopped medium green bell pepper

2 finely chopped culantro leaves

2 garlic cloves

½ teaspoon thyme

Salt and pepper to taste

Preparation:

Soak lentils overnight; drain and cook in 5 cups of water 1½ hours.

Add the rest of ingredients in the last 30 minutes and finish the cooking process.

TIPS: If using a pressure cooker add all ingredients and cook 20 to 25 minutes.

Lentils and Nut Roast

Serves 8 to 10

Ingredients:

1 cup lentils

¼ cup evaporated milk

½ cup chopped cashews

1½ cups cornflakes

1 egg

¼ cup canola oil

½ teaspoon season salt

Sauce:

1½ cups stew tomatoes

1 tablespoon sugar

1 teaspoon salt

3 tablespoons cornstarch

3 tablespoons water

Preparation:

Soak lentils for 5 hours; drain and cover with water, cook until soft. Set aside to cool.

Add the rest of ingredients and mix.

Place in a 9 x 5-inch greased loaf pan; bake at 350°F for 35 minutes.

Combine all ingredients for sauce and pour over loaf.

Place in oven for 2 minutes and remove.

CULTURAL NOTE: *This is the original recipe of Muriel A. Garden Rogers (Jiwanda's grandmother).*

Red Kidney Beans
(Porotos)

Serves 8 to10

Ingredients:

1 pound kidney beans

1 chopped large onion

1 chopped medium green bell pepper

1 finely chopped culantro leaf

2 garlic cloves

1 tablespoon tomato paste

Salt and pepper to taste

Preparation:

Soak beans overnight.

The next day, drain and cook in 3 cups of water 1½ hours.

Add the rest of ingredients in the last 45 minutes and finish the cooking process.

Serve with white rice.

Pig's Feet and Lima Bean Stew
(Habas can patitas de puerco)

Serves 8 to 10

Ingredients:

1 pound large lima beans

1 pound pig's feet

1 chopped large onion

1 chopped medium red bell pepper

1 finely chopped celery stalk

2 garlic cloves

Cumin to taste

Salt and pepper to taste

Splash annatto oil (for color)

Preparation:

Wash, clean, and scrape any hair from pig's feet.

Soak pig's feet in water and white vinegar for 30 minutes.

Drain and wash pig's feet and lima beans; cook in 4 cups of water.

Add the rest of ingredients when beans are starting to get soft.

Cook until pig's feet and beans are soft.

Serve with rice.

CULTURAL NOTE: *This is a recipe provided by Eleanor O. Gale (Jiwanda's mother).*

TIPS: *Ask the grocery store butcher for pig's feet. Also make sure that pig's feet are cut in pieces*

GROUND FOODS, VEGETABLES, ROOT VEGETABLES, AND TUBERS

Ground foods, vegetables, root vegetables, and tubers are very popular in Panama. Malanga (taro or yauntía) is a tuber with different varieties and it's known in Panama as *ñampí* and *otoe*. Ñame is a long round tuber with brown skin and creamy texture that should not be confused with yam (sweet potato). From our research, we learned that there isn't a true English translation for the word *ñame*. All three starchy roots are edible and can be boiled, fried or baked. *Ñame,* yuca or cassava, *otoe*, and *ñampí* are commonly eaten in soups, stews or one-pot meals, salads, and even desserts. Interestingly, indigenous tribes prefer to boil them, while the rest of Panamanians seem to enjoy them fried and/or boiled. They are also served as small bites or as a side dish, especially fried yuca (see glossary).

Vegetable Rounds
(Frituras de vegetales)

Serves 4 to 6

Ingredients:

1 cup pre-mixed bisquick or pancake mix

¾ cup parmesan cheese

¼ teaspoon pepper

4 stiffly beaten eggs

2 ¾ cups shredded zucchini

1 cup shredded carrot

¼ cup chopped onions

¼ cup margarine or butter

Preparation:

In mixing bowl, stir pancake mix, cheese, and pepper.

Mix with eggs until mixture is moistened.

Add vegetables; mix and make rounds.

In a 10-inch skillet, melt 2 tablespoons of butter for each round.

Cook over medium heat about 3 minutes on each side, or until done.

Yuca al Mojo

Serves 4 to 6

Ingredients:

1 pound yuca

3 tablespoons lime juice

4 tablespoons olive oil

4 minced garlic cloves

3 tablespoons finely chopped parsley

Salt to taste

Preparation:

Wash and peel yuca. Cut in large sticks and boil in plenty water with salt.

Lightly fry garlic in oil and add lime juice and salt to taste.

Pour mix over yuca and mix carefully, making sure yuca does not break up.

Sprinkle parsley over yuca and serve.

Yuca Stew
(Guiso de yuca)

Serves 8 to 10

Ingredients:

4 pounds yuca

2 pounds lean pork

2 packets sazón with culantro and achiote (like Goya)

1 tablespoon ground black pepper

2 chicken bouillon cubes

2 julienned red peppers

2 tablespoons canola oil

5 chopped culantro leaves or ½ bunch *recao verde*

1½ cups water

Preparation:

Wash, peel, and cut yuca into 2 or 3-inch strips (see tips under "Yuca Salad with Egg" recipe).

Cut pork into 1½ -inch cubes and brown in oil; add all ingredients but yuca.

When pork is done, add water. Bring it to a boil and add yuca strips. Cook over medium-low heat until yuca is soft.

Serve immediately.

Yuca Pot Pie
(Pastel de yuca)

Serves 6 to 8

Ingredients:

2 pounds yuca

1 pound ground beef

½ pound ground pork

¼ teaspoon oregano

¼ cup chopped large onion

¼ cup chopped peppers

½ cup seeded and chopped tomato

½ cup raisins

2 culantro leaves

1 tablespoon tomato paste

1 tablespoon canola oil

¼ cup water

Salt and pepper to taste

Preparation:

Peel and cut yuca (see tips under "Yuca Salad with Egg" recipe).

To make yuca dough, boil yuca, culantro, and salt until yuca is soft; drain and then grind in a food processor or a grinder. Set aside.

Heat oil in skillet; add beef, pork, and water; cook until done.

Add all ingredients, except yuca.

Cook until most of the sauce has been absorbed. Mixture must be juicy, not dry.

Place most of yuca dough over the bottom and sides of a round baking pan. Put all mixture over yuca dough. Top pie with remaining yuca dough, seal the edges of the pie, and cut slits into the top dough.

Bake pie at 350°F 25 to 30 minutes, or until lightly browned.

Serve hot or cold.

Fried Yuca
(Yuca frita)

Serves 6

Ingredients:

2 pounds yuca

Salt to taste

Canola oil (for frying)

Preparation:

Wash and peel yuca (see tips under "Yuca Salad with Egg" recipe).

Put yuca in a large pot with 4 quarts of water; add salt and boil 35 to 40 minutes, or until soft. Drain and set aside to cool.

Cut yuca into 3-inch long strips and deep-fly. Drain over paper towel.

Sprinkle more salt, if desired.

Serve hot as appetizer or as a side dish.

Otoe Fritters
(Fritura de Otoe)

Serves 4 to 6

Ingredients:

1 pound otoe

1 teaspoon salt

1 garlic clove

1 teaspoon vinegar

1 tablespoon chopped fresh parsley

Canola oil (for frying)

Preparation:

Peel otoe and cut into small pieces.

Use a food processor or a blender to mix otoe and all ingredients (but oil), until mixture is foamy.

Heat oil in skillet and drop mixture by the tablespoonful, frying only a few at a time. Fry 3 to 4 minutes, or until lightly browned on both sides; drain over paper towels.

This dish can be served as a snack or as a side dish. Serve while hot.

Ñame Fritters
(Fritura de Ñame)

Serves 4 to 6

Ingredients:

1 pound ñame

1 egg

1 teaspoon salt

1 teaspoon anise seeds

2 tablespoons flour

Canola oil (for frying)

Preparation:

Wash, peel, cut, and grate ñame.

Add egg, salt, anise seeds, and flour. Mix to obtain stiff dough, add more flour if necessary.

Divide dough into rounds before shaping it into small balls.

Deep-fry dough rounds 3 to 4 minutes, or until lightly browned; drain over paper towel.

Serve hot as appetizer or side dish.

NOTE*: before peeling ñame, read note under "Chicken Sancocho" recipe.*

Ñame Round Fry
(Ñame frito)

Serves 4 to 6

Ingredients:

2 pounds ñame

Salt to taste

Canola oil (for frying)

Preparation:

Peel and wash ñame well.

Cut into rounds and season to taste with salt.

Deep-fry rounds for 3 minutes, or until lightly browned on both sides.

Serve hot as appetizer or as side dish.

Ñame Torte
(Torta de Ñame)

Serves 4

Ingredients:

1 pound ñame

½ cup raisins

3 eggs

3 tablespoons sugar

Preparation:

Boil ñame until soft and mash while it is still hot.

Beat eggs and mix with ñame; add raisins and sugar. Mix well.

Put mixture in a buttered baking dish and dot with butter.

Bake at 350°F 20 to 30 minutes.

Serve as snack or dessert.

Malanga, Otoe and Ñame Pudding

(Pudín de ñampí, otoe y ñame)

Serves 8 to 10

Ingredients:

2 pounds malanga

2 pounds ñame

2 pounds otoe

3 cups fresh coconut milk

3 pounds sugar

5 teaspoons pure vanilla extract

2 teaspoons ground cinnamon

3 teaspoons baking powder

1½ cups raisins

3-4 pounds All-purpose flour

A pinch salt

Preparation:

Grate malanga, otoe, and ñame; combine in the same mixing bowl.

Separately, mix coconut milk and flour; add the root mixture and mix well.

Add raisins, vanilla, sugar, baking powder, cinnamon, and salt. Work the dough for a few minutes, until smooth.

Place dough on baking pan and bake at 350°F 40 to 50 minutes. Brush some melted butter over the top (optional).

Serve cold.

Mashed Malanga
(Puré de Ñampí)

Serves 4 to 6

Ingredients:

2 pounds malanga or ñampí

1 can (12 ounces) evaporated milk

8 tablespoons salted butter

Salt to taste

Preparation:

Peel and cut ñampí into cubes; boil until soft.

Mash with a potato masher and add milk, butter, and salt to taste. Mix well.

Serve hot or warm.

Mashed Ñame
(Puré de Ñame)

Serves 4 to 6

Ingredients:

2 pounds ñame

1 can (12 ounces) evaporated milk

8 tablespoons salted butter

Salt to taste

Preparation:

Peel and cut ñame into cubes; boil until soft.

Mash with a potato masher and add milk, butter, and salt to taste. Mix well.

Serve hot or warm.

Mashed Otoe
(Puré de Otoe)

Serves 4 to 6

Ingredients:

2 pounds otoe

1 can (12 ounces) evaporated milk

8 tablespoons salted butter

Salt to taste

Preparation:

Peel and cut otoe into cubes; boil until soft.

Mash with a potato masher and add milk, butter, and salt to taste. Mix well.

Serve hot or warm.

Picadillo de Ahuyama

Serves 4

Ingredients:

2 cups cubed pumpkin or squash

1 tablespoon vinegar

1 chopped green or red bell pepper

1 chopped medium onion

1 chopped celery stalk

½ cup salted butter

1 tablespoon All-purpose seasoning (like Goya)

2 teaspoons Worcestershire sauce

1 can (6 ounces) evaporated milk

Garlic powder to taste

1 cup water

Preparation:

Heat butter over medium-low heat to fry pumpkin; add water and cook for 20 minutes.

Add the rest of ingredients; mix, cover, and cook 20 to 25 additional minutes.

Serve with white rice.

CULTURAL NOTE: *The Webster's New International Dictionary defines pumpkin as "a gourd-like fruit of a vine (Cucurbita pepo) widely cultivated as food for stock, as a vegetable, and for making pumpkin pies... the majority of pumpkins are nearly round in shape and deep yellow in color." There is an enormous variety of pumpkins. In Panama, pumpkin or squash is best known as ahuyama or zapallo and is commonly used in salads, soups, stews, pies, and sweets*

POULTRY

C hicken is the most common type of poultry in the world and Panama is not the exception. Panamanian families select chicken as main dish for obvious reasons: it's economical and versatile, and when prepared well, it's tasty and healthy. Chicken is the basic ingredient in a wide variety of Panamanian dishes: fried chicken, oven roasted or baked chicken, grilled chicken, braised or stewed chicken, chicken casseroles or skillet chicken, just to mention a few. Panamanians also like to make chicken broths and soups (see sections under **SOUPS AND ONE-POT MEALS**). Even though most Panamanians eat more chicken than other poultry, one can find a few other types of poultry in recipes, like duck and turkey; and game birds, like quail, and Cornish game hen. All of them are available at supermarkets or are served at restaurants. For instance, duck can be homemade and/or served at some Asian restaurants. Turkey can be as delicious and versatile as chicken. Panamanians usually prepare it for Christmas, since they do not celebrate "Thanksgiving." Cooking turkey for the holidays is an American tradition that was passed on to Panamanians. Turkey recipes are inspired by Americans who lived for many years in the Canal Zone area. There is another Panamanian turkey recipe inspired by the Panamanian-Chinese cuisine, since one of the major ingredients is soy sauce or *salsa china*. Other simple wild bird recipes may be found among farmers and indigenous tribes. Obviously, these types of birds are not available in local grocery stores or supermarkets. Some of these wild bird recipes have been passed down through generations of Panamanian families.

Roasted Chicken
(Pollo asado)

Serves 6 to 8

Ingredients:

1 4-pound chicken

3 minced garlic cloves

1 cup flour

½ tablespoon paprika

½ cup butter

Salt and pepper to taste

Preparation:

Cut chicken in small pieces and season with garlic, salt, and pepper.

Dip pieces in melted butter.

Mix flour and paprika; roll pieces of chicken in mixture.

Place pieces of chicken skin side up in greased large shallow baking pan.

Bake at 350° F about 1 hour.

Pan-Fried Chicken
(Pollo apanado)

Serves 4

Ingredients:

2 pounds boneless skinless chicken breast

4 minced garlic cloves

1 chopped medium onion

3 tablespoons canola oil

1 cup All-purpose flour

Adobo All-purpose seasoning (like Goya)

Salt and pepper to taste

Preparation:

Wash and butterfly chicken breasts.

Mix oil, onion, and garlic.

Season chicken with adobo, salt, and pepper; marinate for 30 minutes.

Heat oil in skillet over medium-low.

Coat chicken with flour and pan-fry until fully cooked and crust is golden brown and crispy.

Fried Chicken
(Pollo frito)

Serves 6

Ingredients:

3 pounds cut up chicken

3 minced garlic cloves

3 tablespoons salt

Ground black pepper to taste

Canola oil (for frying)

Preparation:

In a mixing bowl, combine garlic, salt, and pepper; rub mixed ingredients inside and out of chicken. Refrigerate about 1 hour.

Heat oil in a medium cast iron skillet over medium-high; Deep-fry chicken for 35 minutes, turning to brown evenly.

Stuffed Baked Chicken
(Pollo relleno)

Serves 6

Ingredients:

1 ready to cook whole chicken (3-4 pounds)

3 minced garlic cloves

3 teaspoons salt

½ teaspoon powdered marjoram

1 chopped medium red onion

¼ cup annatto oil

Ingredients for stuffing:

1 pound ground pork

3 tablespoons butter

3 tablespoons tomato sauce

1 tablespoon raisins

½ cup chopped olives

Preparation:

Mix salt, garlic, marjoram, and onions; rub chicken inside and out with mixed ingredients 1 hour before stuffing. Store chicken in a cool place.

Stuffing:

Add all ingredients for stuffing to ground pork and mix well.

Stuff chicken and brush annatto oil over it.

Cook in the oven at 350°F for 2 hours, or until done.

Panamanian-Style Christmas Turkey
(Pavo navideño)

Serves 16 to 20

Ingredients:

1 20-pound turkey

1 bottle (10 ounces) soy sauce

2 small cooking syringes

Ingredients for stuffing

½ pound lean ground beef

2 medium size diced potatoes

1 can (14.5 ounces) mixed vegetables

Salt and pepper to taste

Preparation:

Inject turkey 24 hours before cooking. Place in oven bag and refrigerate overnight.

The next day, re-inject with accumulated juice in bag (use second cooking syringe).

Make stuffing: Mix ground beef, potatoes, vegetables, salt, and pepper to taste; insert stuffing in turkey.

Put turkey in roasting pan; place in a preheated 400°F oven.

Cook turkey at 350° F for 4 hours.

CULTURAL NOTE: This is the original recipe of Xenia Gutiérrez (Nilsa's oldest sister). This turkey is served as a main dish for Christmas and/or New Year's celebrations at many Panamanian homes. The American and Chinese influences are very evident, since eating turkey for the holidays is very American and using soy sauce is very Chinese.

Chicken in Coconut Sauce
(Pollo en salsa de coco)

Serves 6

Ingredients:

6 chicken breasts

2 tablespoons canola oil

1 julienned red pepper

2 cups fresh coconut milk

1 cup parmesan cheese

2 teaspoons salt

1 teaspoon ground black pepper

Preparation:

Heat oil in skillet; cook and stir chicken.

In a bowl, mix coconut milk with cheese and heat at low temperature until it thickens.

Cook and stir red pepper and add chicken; combine with coconut mixture.

Add salt and pepper; mix well.

Serve with rice or over cooked pasta.

Ginger Chicken
(Pollo con jengibre)

Serves 6

Ingredients:

½ pound boneless and skinless chicken breast

1 minced garlic clove

2 tablespoons fish sauce

1 tablespoon oyster sauce

1 tablespoon sugar

¼ cup green bell pepper

¼ cup red bell pepper

¼ cup mushrooms

¼ cup sliced onion

¼ cup grated ginger

1 tablespoon canola oil

½ teaspoon ground white pepper

Preparation:

Heat oil in a wok or a skillet; add chicken and garlic, cook for 10 minutes.

Add the rest of ingredients and cook for 3 additional minutes, stirring frequently.

Serve immediately.

BBQ Chicken
(Pollo a la barbacoa)

Serves 6 to 8

Ingredients:

4 pounds chicken

½ teaspoon pepper

½ teaspoon ginger powder

½ tablespoon curry powder

¾ pound pitted olives

1 teaspoon barbecue sauce

2 pounds margarine or butter

½ cup cherry syrup

Salt to taste

Preparation:

Start the barbecue grill and heat to about 275°F.

Take the skin off chicken and get rid of chicken fat; debone and cut into 1½ pieces and season with ginger, curry powder, pepper, and barbecue sauce.

Place an olive on the grill followed by a piece of chicken. Repeat the process until all chicken is gone.

In a pot, melt margarine and cherry syrup (keep the mix hot).

Raise the barbecue grill to eight inches above the fire; cook chicken until brown on both sides.

Brush chicken with margarine and syrup mixture; continue to cook chicken until done.

This recipe can be made in the oven in a glass dish or a baking pan (350°F).

Rincón Tableño Chicken
(Gallina Rincón Tableño)

Serves 6

Ingredients:

3 pounds chicken pieces with bone

8 minced garlic cloves

1 chopped large onion

2 chopped green peppers

4 finely chopped culantro leaves

1 (2.11 ounces) packet or ¼ cup chicken *consumé* (like Knorr or Maggi)

2 (.81 ounces) chicken bouillon cubes (like Knorr or Maggi)

Salt and ground black pepper to taste

2 tablespoons canola oil

Preparation:

Season chicken with chicken consomé, salt, black pepper, chicken bouillon cubes, garlic, onion, culantro, and green peppers. Marinate chicken for 30 minutes.

Heat oil in skillet; cook chicken on medium-low, flipping pieces constantly until done.

Serve immediately.

Stew Chicken
(Guiso de pollo)

Serves 8

Ingredients:

4 pounds chicken pieces with or without skin

1 chopped large green bell pepper

1 chopped large red pepper

1 chopped large onion

3 garlic cloves

2 packs sazón with culantro

1 can (6 ounces) tomato sauce

1 tablespoon tomato paste

6 tablespoons Worcestershire

6 tablespoons soy sauce

2 tablespoons Ají chombo (or habanero pepper)

¼ cup oil

½ cup water

Garlic powder to taste

Ground black pepper to taste

Preparation:

Season chicken with black pepper, garlic powder, 1 pack of sazón, 3 tablespoons Worcestershire sauce, and 3 tablespoons soy sauce. Let marinate for 1 hour.

Heat oil in a large skillet; add garlic cloves and brown chicken pieces (remove garlic cloves before adding chicken). Set chicken aside.

In the same skillet, cook and stir onion and peppers 5 minutes.

Add the rest of soy and Worcestershire sauces, and remaining sazón.

Add tomato sauce, tomato paste, and water (add more water if needed without diluting the taste).

Add chicken to sauce, cover and cook for 30 minutes, or until chicken is fully cooked.

French-Panamanian Quail
(Codorniz a la panameño-francesa)

Serves 4

Ingredients:

4 quails

2 ½ tablespoons butter

1 chopped large onion

1 tablespoon All-purpose flour

1 cup white wine or red cooking wine

1 cup veal or beef stock

½ pound trimmed and halved assorted mushrooms

½ cup chopped fresh parsley

Salt to taste

Freshly ground black pepper to taste

Splash olive oil

Preparation:

Clean and tie up quail; season to taste with salt and pepper.

Melt ½ of butter and pour a drop of oil in a large cast iron skillet; brown quail on all sides over medium-high heat.

Remove and set aside.

Cook and stir onion until golden (use the same skillet).

Stir the flour into onion; cook for 1 minute and remove.

Deglaze the skillet with wine, stirring up the good bits on the bottom of the skillet with a wooden spoon.

Return quail and onion to the skillet. Pour over stock, cover, and simmer for about 25 minutes, or until quail is just cooked through and the thin consistency of sauce is reduced. Don't let dry.

In a separate skillet, while quail is cooking, heat remaining butter and cook mushrooms 5 to 8 minutes. Season mushrooms with salt and pepper; toss them all together with chopped parsley. Remove from stove.

When quail is done, add cooked mushrooms with parsley to sauce.

Tilt into a serving dish, set quail on top, and serve.

TIPS: *Homemade veal or beef stock is preferred. Making stock at home is very time consuming. It could take up to 12 hours. Luckily for us, today there are commercial products on the market that are almost as good as making them ourselves.*

SEAFOOD

Seafood has been so plentiful in Panama that most people believe that a village populated by fishermen came up with the name "Panama" which means "many fish or abundance of fish." Others believe that the origin of the name "Panama" comes from a commonly found species of tree; others believe that "Panama" is an indigenous word and it means "many butterflies." Traditionally, this nation's subsistence agriculture never depended exclusively on corn. In Panama, game and fish were always sources of protein.

Panama is definitely a paradise for seafood lovers! Seafood dishes are traditionally familiar in Panama. Seafood is excellent and in abundance throughout the nation: fish, shrimp, lobster, octopus, shark, crab, snail, and many others. Seafood is certainly a staple in the national diet. Traditional Panamanian seafood dishes come five ways: fried, grilled, al ajillo (with a spicy garlic sauce), in soups (see section for soups), or *a la española* (sautéed with tomatoes and onions). One of Panama's favorite appetizers is ceviche (made of fish, shrimp, octopus, shark or a combination of some of them). This recipe can be found under APPETIZERS AND LITTLE BITES.

Seafood in Sauce

(Zarzuela)

Serves 6 to 8

Ingredients:

1 ½ pounds coarsely chopped octopus

2 pounds red snapper

2 pounds prawns

1 pound clams

2 pounds coarsely chopped and cleaned squid

1 habanero pepper (or Scotch bonnet pepper)

1 cup chopped onions

½ cup chopped green bell peppers

4 chopped celery stalks

2 chopped large carrots

6 minced garlic cloves

8 chopped medium red tomatoes

1 bay leaf

2 tablespoons salt

1 cup white wine

2 cups fish broth

¼ cup olive oil

2 cups water

Preparation:

Cook red snapper's heads in 2 cups of water to make fish broth.

Heat oil; cook and stir onion, bell pepper, garlic, and tomatoes for 5 minutes.

Wash and clean seafood well. Add octopus, pieces of fish, whole prawns, clams, squid, and habanero pepper. Let cook for10 minutes.

Add salt, wine, fish broth, carrots, bay leaf, and celery; cook, uncovered, until mixture boils.

Cover and simmer 10 to 15 minutes. Do not let dry.

If desired, add more salt and pepper to taste. Serve hot with white rice.

Tropical Lobster

(Langosta tropical)

Serves 4

Ingredients

4 (1½ -pound) live tropical lobsters

4 cups water

2 tablespoons salt

Preparation

Bring water and salt to a boil in a 5-gallon stockpot. Add lobster; cover and steam 14 minutes, or until it turns red.

Serve with melted butter or coconut dipping sauce (see Coconut Dipping Sauce recipe).

Lacro Kuna Yala

Serves 4

Ingredients:

1 ½ pounds fish (flounder, cod or haddock)

2 tomatoes

2 green plantains

1 large onion

Seasoned salt to taste

2 lemons

½ cup flour

Salt and black pepper to taste

1 cup water

Preparation:
Clean fish and cut into 2 to 3-inch pieces.
Add salt and pepper, seasoned salt, and lemon juice.
Coat fish with flour and deep-fry until golden brown
Peel plantains; grind or blend in a food processor.
Use blender or food processor to prepare a sauce with onion and tomatoes.
Place plantain in skillet and add salt, pepper, and water. Cover and cook on medium-low heat 10 to 15 minutes.
Add sauce, stir, cover, and simmer for 15 minutes.
Serve fried fish and plantain mix together.

Tule Masi 1

Serves 6 to 8

Ingredients:

1 grated fresh coconut

6 peeled ripe plantains

1 fish, crab or lobster

3-4 cups water

1 hot pepper (optional)

1 lemon (optional)

Salt to taste

Preparation

Strain coconut milk with water. Pour half of coconut milk
in cooking pan and boil plantains. Pour the other half of
coconut milk in a different cooking pan and boil seafood of
your choice (fish, crab or lobster).

Add salt, lemon juice, and hot pepper to plantains (it will
look like plantain soup).

Prepare and eat dish, mixing a spoon of plantain broth with a
spoon of cooked seafood.

Tule Masi 2

(a variation of previous recipe)

Serves 6 to 8

Ingredients:

2 pounds fish (cleaned and cut in pieces)

1 medium finely chopped onion

1 minced garlic clove

2 cups peeled and cubed ñame

2 cups peeled and cubed yuca

2 cups peeled and cubed otoe

6 cups coconut milk

Salt to taste

Lime (for serving)

Hot pepper

Preparation:

In a large soup pot, add coconut milk, otoe, and yuca and cook for 15 minutes; add ñame and cook for 30 additional minutes, or until soft.

Add salt to taste, onion, and garlic.

Add fish to the pot and cook until done.

Serve with lime and hot pepper on the side.

Fried Whole Corvina

(Corvina frita)

Serves 1

Ingredients:

1 whole Corvina

3 chopped garlic cloves

1 teaspoon salt (or to taste)

¼ teaspoon pure ground black pepper

¼ cup flour

Preparation:
Clean and wash Corvina.

In a platter, combine flour with garlic, salt, and pepper.

Double dip both sides of fish in bowl and make sure it is covered with seasoning.

Deep-fry in hot oil until lightly browned.

Let stand 3 to 5 minutes and serve with vegetable and coconut rice.

Garlic Shrimp
(Camarones al ajillo)

Serves 4

Ingredients:

4 tablespoons butter

6 finely chopped garlic cloves

2 pounds large or medium fresh shrimp

(or frozen uncooked shrimp)

1 tablespoon lemon juice

½ teaspoon lemon zest

½ cup water

½ tablespoon salt (or to taste)

½ teaspoon seasoned salt

¼ cup finely chopped fresh culantro

¼ cup finely chopped parsley

Dash your favorite hot sauce (or Ají chombo)

Preparation:

Wash shrimp (defrost if frozen) and take heads and shells off.

Heat butter in a large skillet on low; cook garlic in melted butter, stirring for 2 minutes.

Increase the heat to medium-low; add shrimp, water, lemon juice, lemon zest, salt, seasoned salt, culantro, and parsley.

Cook for 6 minutes, stirring, until they turn pink. Serve immediately, accompanied by rice and vegetables.

Stuffed Fish
(Pescado relleno)

Serves 4
Ingredients:
1 (2-3 pounds) snapper
3 hot peppers or chile peppers
10 limes
10 garlic cloves
½ pound flour
Parsley to taste
Curry powder to taste
Salt and black pepper to taste

Preparation:
Clean fish with 5 limes. Then, season fish with curry powder, salt, and black pepper; place in refrigerator for about 6 to 8 hours, or overnight.

Finely chop the rest of ingredients and stuff fish. Reserve 4 garlic cloves.

Flour fish and fry in hot oil with reserved garlic cloves until golden brown.

Remove fish from oil and serve hot with the rest of limes.

NOTE: Ají chombo is the hot pepper of choice in Panama.

TIPS: For better results, cut fish into 3-inch pieces and make small holes for stuffing, then flour and fry.

Panamanian-Style Bacalao
(Bacalao panameño)

Serves 4

Ingredients:

2 pounds bacalao

1 pound potatoes

2 minced garlic cloves

1 finely chopped large onion

1 chopped large red bell pepper

1 can (6 ounces) tomato paste

5 chopped culantro leaves

Curry powder to taste

Black pepper to taste

1 cup water (from potatoes)

3 tablespoons vegetable oil

Preparation:

Soak salted cod in warm water for 1 hour; drain water from cod and soak for 8 hours in cool water.

Next day, drain water again and flake cod, making sure there are no bones.

Peel and boil potatoes and cut into cubes. Reserve 1 cup of water from potatoes.

Heat oil in a large skillet; cook and stir onion, peppers, black pepper, culantro, curry powder and garlic. Fry for 5 minutes and add tomato paste and water.

Add bacalao to mix and cook for 10 additional minutes.

Add potatoes to bacalao; mix and cook on low until sauce is cooked.

TIPS: The bacalao is usually served over rice.

Escovitch or Escoviched Fish

(Escabeche de pescado)

Serves 10

Ingredients:

3 pounds Corvina

2 garlic cloves

4 limes

1 cup white vinegar

2 large thinly sliced onions

1 tablespoon allspice berries

1-2 Scotch bonnet peppers (optional)

2 chopped small red bell peppers

2 tablespoons salt

1 teaspoon ground black pepper

½ cup of canola oil

Flour

Preparation:
Clean and wash fish with limes and water. Dry fish and cut into 2-inch pieces.

In a large plate, combine flour, salt, and pepper. Then lightly coat each piece of fish with the mix.

Heat oil in skillet; add garlic cloves. Remove garlic cloves when brown.

Fry fish in the skillet until lightly browned and drain on paper towels.

In a non-reactive sauce pan, combine vinegar, peppers, onions, and allspice; simmer until onion is translucent.

Place fish in a glass dish or a glass baking pan; pour sauce with onions over fish, cover and set aside to cool.

Let stand for 5 minutes and serve with vegetable and coconut rice.

Fish can also be refrigerated overnight and served the next day.

TIPS: *You can add 1 seeded hot pepper to give the fish some flavor without a lot of heat.*

Rondon
(Rondón de pescado)

Serves 6

Ingredients:

2 pounds cleaned and cut red or yellow snapper pieces

1 chopped medium onion

1 minced garlic clove

6 chopped culantro leaves

2 chopped large red bell peppers

1 pound peeled and cubed ñame

1 pound peeled and cubed yuca

1 grated coconut

½ pound flour

1 liter chicken stock

1 teaspoon black pepper

Salt to taste

Canola oil (for frying)

Preparation:

Deep-fry fish until brown; drain on paper towels.

In a large soup pot, bring chicken stock to a boil; add ñame and yuca. Lower heat to medium-low, cover and cook.

Add water in small amounts to flour.

Make small finger-length dumplings and add them to the pot. Add onion, red peppers, garlic, culantro, pepper, and salt to the soup.

Make coconut milk by adding boiling water to grated coco to make two cups.

Add fry fish to soup and cook for 5 minutes.

Add coconut milk and cook for 10 additional minutes and serve.

Octopus in Coconut Sauce
(Pulpo en salsa de coco)

Serves 8

Ingredients:

7 pounds octopus

1 large coconut; coconut cream

1 pack annatto seeds

2 chopped green peppers

2 minced garlic cloves

4 culantro leaves

1 pinch oregano

Preparation:

Wash and boil octopus, let cool; clean and chop in small pieces.

Boil octopus again for 45 minutes; when tender, add garlic, culantro, green peppers, and coconut cream.

Prepare annatto seeds in two tablespoons oil in a small skillet. Strain and discard seeds.

Add oregano and annatto oil to octopus; simmer until liquid is consumed.

Codfish and Ackee
(Bacalao con akí)

Serves 4

Ingredients:

½ pound boneless bacalao (salt cod)

1 can (15 ounces) drained ackee

1 minced garlic clove

1 sliced large onion

½ chopped large red or green bell pepper

¼ finely chopped Scotch bonnet pepper

1 teaspoon tomato paste

Salt and black pepper to taste

3 tablespoons oil

Preparation:

Heat oil in a 9-inch skillet; add onions, bell pepper; Scotch bonnet, garlic, and tomato paste.

Cook for a few minutes; add codfish to mix.

Add ackee; cook for a few minutes and add pepper and taste for salt (add more if needed).

Serve hot with root vegetables and dumplings or rice.

CULTURAL NOTE: *This recipe is based on the original recipe from Jamaica; and it is a staple recipe of Afro-Panamanians from Caribbean descent.*

TIPS: *Soak salted cod in warm water for 1 hour. Drain water from cod and soak 8 hours in cool water. Drain water from cod and flake, making sure there are no bones.*

Fufu

Serves 6

Ingredients:

5 pounds fish

¼ pound green plantain

1/3 pound green banana

2 pounds ñame

4 pounds yuca

2 pounds ñampí (malanga)

2 pounds otoe

4 grated coconuts

1 chopped large onion

6 chopped culantro leaves

1 chopped small red bell pepper

3 minced garlic cloves

1 teaspoon annatto oil

Canola oil (for frying)

Salt and black pepper to taste

Oregano to taste

Scotch bonnet pepper or Ají chombo to taste

Preparation:

Wash and clean fish.
Peel and cut vegetables and bananas into cubes and place them in water until ready to use.

Make the coconut milk by adding warm water to the grated coconut. Strain the coconut milk into a large pot; add onion, garlic, chopped culantro, and bell pepper. Boil and add root vegetables, plantains, and bananas.

Meanwhile, deep-fry fish until brown; drain on paper towels.

Add fish to soup, annatto oil, oregano, and salt and pepper to taste. Continue to boil soup until vegetables are soft.

Add cut and seeded Scotch bonnet pepper to soup.

Serve hot.

Clams in Red Sauce
(Almejas en salsa roja)

Serves 4 to 6

Ingredientes:

1 pound clams

1 finely chopped medium onion

¼ teaspoon oregano

1 finely chopped tomato

1 tablespoon tomato paste

1 tablespoon canola oil

1 cup water

Salt and pepper to taste

Ají chombo sauce to taste

Preparation:

Heat oil in skillet; add tomato and onion. Cook and stir for 5 minutes.

Add tomato paste, clams, oregano, and pepper.

Mix and add water, salt and hot sauce to taste.

Cook 10 to 15 minutes, until clams are opened.

Guacho de Mariscos

Serves 6 to 8

Ingredients:

2 pounds clams

2 pounds calamari

2 pounds cleaned, deveined and chopped shrimp

2 cleaned and chopped lobsters

1 pound chopped scallops

½ cup olive oil

1 cup chopped onions

½ cup chopped peppers

4 minced garlic cloves

2 cups chopped tomatoes

2 culantro leaves

2 laurel leaves

1 cup red wine

1 habanero pepper (or ají chombo)

10 cups water

4 cups rice

1 tablespoon salt

Preparation:

Heat oil in a large pot; add onion, peppers, and garlic, then stir and fry.

Add tomatoes and cook for 5 minutes.

Stir vegetables; add culantro leaves, laurel leaves, and wine.

Add clam, shrimp, lobster, calamari, and scallops.

Add previously washed rice, salt, and water.

Add ají chombo (remove before it bursts) and reduce heat; cover and cook until most of the water is absorbed and rice is cooked.

Tapao Garachineño

Serves 4 to 6

Ingredients:

3 pounds red snapper

2 green plantains

2 ripe plantains

5 chopped culantro leaves

2 large tomatoes

1 large onion

4 garlic cloves

2 green peppers

1 tablespoon soy sauce

1 cup chicken broth

½ cup water

2 tablespoons canola oil

½ cup lemon juice

Salt and ground black pepper to taste

Preparation:

Marinate fish in lemon juice and soy sauce for 35 minutes; season with black pepper and fry.

Remove and discard pepper and tomato seeds. Blend peppers and tomatoes to make sauce; add this sauce to fish. Keep warm in oven.

Peel, cut, and boil plantains separately; add culantro and salt to taste.

Chopped the rest of ingredients; cook and stir.

Add chicken broth and water. Mix well.

Add mixture to fish and serve immediately with boiled plantains on the side.

Conch in Ginger Sauce
(Cambombia con salsa de jengibre)

Serves 8

Ingredients:

2 pounds conch

4 pieces ginger

4 minced garlic cloves

2 chicken bouillon cubes

2 tablespoons flour

¼ cup soy sauce

1 can (14 ounces) green peas

Preparation:

Soften conch with a mallet and cut in pieces.

In a large pot put conch and ginger to boil. While conch is boiling, add garlic and chicken bouillon and cook for 5 minutes.

Dilute flour in soy sauce and add to conch. Continue to cook over low heat, stirring until sauce thickens.

Remove ginger and add can of peas and serve.

Chinese-Style Spider Crab
(Centollo al estilo chino)

Serves 6 to 8

Ingredients:

3-4 pounds spider crab

2-3 ounces thinly sliced ginger

4 culantro leaves

1 ají chombo (optional)

3 minced garlic cloves

1 tablespoon salt

1 teaspoon sugar

1 teaspoon cornstarch

½ cup water

1 serving spoon canola oil

1 bunch scallion (optional)

Preparation:

Clean spider crab and cut in large pieces.

Heat oil in a wok; add garlic, ginger, culantro, and ají chombo. Fry for 5 seconds.

Add crab and cook 5 to 10 minutes.

Add salt, sugar, and water if needed; cover and cook for approximately 5 minutes.

Uncover wok; add scallion and cornstarch (dissolve cornstarch in three teaspoons of water). Mix until sauce thickens.

Serve hot.

PORK,
BEEF,
AND OTHER
MEATS

E uropeans and Americans transformed Panamanian cuisine, imposing a meat diet and a "canned and preserved food" type of culture. Pork and beef are cooked in many different ways. Like in the U.S., meats can be eaten broiled, smoked and cured, grilled, braised, pan-fried, stewed or roasted, just to mention a few. Some Panamanian pork and beef recipes are reminiscent of the gastronomy from the southern region of the U.S., with the added Panamanian flavor, of course. In rural Panama, it is normal to eat wild animal meats, such as rabbit, iguana, agouti or ñeque.

Roast Pork
(Lechón asado)

Serves 15 to 20

Ingredients:

1 30-pound pork

2 beef bouillon cubes

2 minced garlic cloves

½ cup annatto oil

½ cup chopped culantro

½ cup sour orange juice

½ cup pineapple juice

3 tablespoons salt

Black pepper to taste

Preparation:

In a blender, combine pepper, salt, garlic, bouillon cubes, culantro, and annatto oil to obtain a pasty mixture.

Mix juices and paste, then marinate pork for 24 hours.

Put pork in a large oven pan. Place in oven, cover, and cook at 350°F 3½ to 4 hours.

Let it cook, uncovered, for 30 additional minutes.

Pork Sausage
(Chorizo de puerco)

Serves 24 to 30

Ingredients:

3 pounds lean pork

3 tablespoons salt

1 teaspoon ground black pepper

6 minced garlic cloves

1 teaspoon powdered marjoram or dried oregano

½ cup annatto oil

2 yards dry pork intestines

Preparation:

Cut pork into 1-inch cubes; add all ingredients, except for intestines, and mix well.

Stuff intestines using a wide and long funnel, twisting and tying off sausage links every 4 inches. Pierce sausage to allow some fat to drain out.

Boil sausage 3 to 5 minutes and hang it up to dry.

These sausages are great grilled!

Refrigerate or freeze newly made sausages, if you don't plan to cook them right away.

TIPS: *Clean pork intestines. Before stuffing, fill them with air and hang them up to dry so they will not stick.*

Christmas Pork Roast
(Lomo de puerco navideño)

Serves 10 to 12

Ingredients:

1 4-pound pork roast

8 minced garlic cloves

2 pounds brown sugar

2 teaspoons salt

2 cups coca cola

½ cup raisins

2 green apples

10 seedless prunes

Preparation:

Trim off excess fat from pork; puncture 10 holes in pork with knife and place prunes in holes. Set aside.

Mix garlic, salt, sugar, and coca cola; rub mixture all over pork.

Put pork in a large oven pan. Place in oven, cover and cook at 350°F 2 to 3 hours.

Uncover pork; add raisins and place apple slices around pork.

Cook for an additional 15 minutes.

Remove from oven; cut into thin slices and serve.

Christmas Ham
(Jamón navideño)

Serves 18 to 20

Ingredients:

1 12-pound ham

2 (1-liter) bottle *coca cola*

4 cups water

40 whole cloves

1 pineapple

1½ cups brown sugar

1 (10-ounce) jar cherries

Preparation:

In a large pot, add *coca cola*, water, and ham; cook for 1 hour.

Remove ham and place on a large oven pan.

With a knife, puncture holes in different places of ham.

Place whole cloves in holes made with knife.

Cook ham in oven at 350°F 2½ to 3 hours. Remove from oven and set aside.

Peel and cut pineapple in slices and remove the center core.

Cover both sides of each slice with brown sugar. Reserve ½ cup for later.

Put pineapple slices on top of ham. Place cherries in the hole of pineapple slices.

Sprinkle reserved brown sugar over ham; put back in oven and cook for 25 minutes.

NOTE: Serve as a side dish for Christmas and/or New Year's Eve celebrations.

Tasajo

Serves 6 to 8

Ingredients:

1 Rump roast

6 garlic cloves

½ teaspoon black pepper

1 teaspoon salt

1 tablespoon Worcestershire sauce

½ cup annatto oil

8 seeded and chopped tomatoes

1 can (15 ounces) peeled tomatoes

1 teaspoon oregano

Preparation:

Trim off any excess fat from roast; cut into 1-inch wide and 4 to 6-inch long strips (see tips).

In a blender, combine garlic, pepper, and salt to obtain a pasty mix.

Add Worcestershire sauce and mix well.

Rub mixture on meat, place it in a large glass bowl; cover and marinate for 4 hours.

Barbecue beef strips on grill until cooked and dried.

Remove dried strips and beat with a kitchen mallet until the fibers are loose, but still in one piece.

Preparing sauce:

Cook and stir chopped tomatoes in annatto oil.

Add the can of tomatoes and with a wooden spoon mash them until well mixed.

In a large skillet, add meat, oregano, and sauce.

Mix well and cook on low for about 10 minutes.

NOTE: Country-style tasajo is dried using a traditional method, hanging beef strips from wires over a fogón (rustic stove or cooking area constructed of bricks or stones). You can also dry tasajo in a smoker.

TIPS: How to cut beef strips? Position the knife on the meat and cut strips with the grain of the meat.

Shredded Beef
(Ropa vieja)

Serves 10 to 12

Ingredients:

1½ pounds flank steak

4 tablespoons canola oil

1 chopped onion

2 chopped garlic cloves

1 can (15.5 ounces) tomato sauce

½ teaspoon ground black pepper

1 teaspoon salt

Preparation:

Heat 1 tablespoon of oil in a skillet to brown flank steak; add water, cover and cook for 3 hours, or until very soft.

Shred meat with your hands.

Heat oil in a medium skillet; cook and stir onion and garlic.

Add tomato sauce, pepper, and salt.

Add sauce to meat. Let meat absorb sauce for 15 minutes.

Beef and Tomato

(Bisté entomatado)

Serves 6 to 8

Ingredients:

2 pounds top round (or large steak)

1 chopped large onion

4 minced garlic cloves

8 chopped pear tomatoes

1 tablespoon Worcestershire sauce

1 tablespoon soy sauce

2 tablespoons canola oil

2 tablespoons annatto oil

1 teaspoon dry oregano

Salt and black pepper to taste

Preparation:

Season and marinate steak with garlic, annatto oil, soy sauce, and Worcestershire sauce for 1 hour.

Heat oil in a large skillet and brown steak on both sides. Do not overcook.

In a different skillet, cook and stir onions and tomatoes; add oregano.

Season to taste with salt and paper.

Put mixture over stake and let cook for 5 additional minutes.

Serve warm.

Beef Stew
(Carne guisada)

Serves 4 to 6

Ingredients:

2 pounds beef (stew meat)

1 can (15 ounces) tomato sauce

1 large onion

4 minced garlic cloves

1½ cups water

2 tablespoons white vinegar

2 tablespoons canola oil

Fresh or dry parsley to taste

Salt and pepper to taste

Preparation:

Heat oil in a skillet; brown meat for 25 minutes.

Add water, vinegar, and tomato sauce. Cover and cook on low for 20 minutes.

Add large chunks of onion, garlic, and parsley.

Season to taste with salt and pepper.

Cover and cook on medium-low for 25 minutes.

Let stand for 5 additional minutes and serve with white rice.

Panamanian-Style Beef
(Bisté picado)

Serves 4

Ingredients:

1 pound beef fillet

1 chopped large onion

1 chopped large green pepper

1 minced garlic clove

1 chopped large tomato

Salt and pepper to taste

Canola oil

Preparation:

Cut beef in small pieces.

Heat oil in a skillet and brown beef.

Cover and cook on low for 5 minutes.

Add onion, green pepper, garlic, and tomato.

Season to taste with salt and pepper.

Cook for 5 additional minutes and serve.

Oxtail
(Rabo de buey)

Serves 6 to 8

Ingredients:

2.5 pounds pre-cut oxtail

¼ cup canola oil

6 cups water

2 chopped medium tomatoes

2 chopped medium onions

3 minced garlic cloves

2 chopped celery stalks

1 tablespoon thyme

3 sliced green bell peppers

2 cans (15.5 ounces) black or red beans

3 tablespoons sea salt

Preparation:
Trim excess fat from around oxtail, then brown in oil (see tips on how to tenderize oxtail).

Place oxtail pieces in a large cooking pot (or pressure cooker). Add 4 cups of water and boil for 35 minutes.

Add tomatoes, onions, garlic cloves, thyme, celery, bell peppers, and salt.

Stir, cover, and boil over medium-low heat until tender. Stir again for a few minutes and let simmer until thick.

Add remaining water and beans.

Lower heat, cover and simmer for 10 minutes.

To spice it up, serve with ají chombo or habanero sauce on the side. More salt can be added to individual servings.

· Serve with white rice.

TIPS: *How to tenderize oxtail?* *Marinate oxtail pieces 8 hours, or overnight in 4 cups of water and ¼ cup of vinegar or papaya extracts.*

If using pressure cooker, cook for about 2 hours.

Beef on the Stick

(Carne en palito)

Serves 6

Ingredients:

1 pound thinly sliced beef (long strips)

2 tablespoons orange juice

1 tablespoon canola oil

6-8 minced garlic cloves

2 tablespoons annatto powder

1 tablespoon cumin

Salt and pepper to taste

6-8 bamboo skewers

Preparation:

Combine orange juice, oil, garlic, annatto, cumin, salt, and pepper to make adobo.

Season meat with adobo and refrigerate for 2 hours.

Slide meat into the bamboo skewers.

Grill 2 to 3 minutes on each side. Baste with your favorite hot sauce and continue turning and basting for 2 additional minutes, or until meat is done.

CULTURAL NOTE: *Carne en Palito is one of Panama's favorite street foods. It is usually sold during carnival celebrations and other popular festivities.*

Salpicón de Carne

Serves 4 to 6

Ingredientes:

1 pound ground beef

1 minced garlic clove

1 minced medium onion

1 boiled medium potato

1 hard-cooked egg

1 boiled carrot

2 tablespoons tomato sauce

2 tablespoons bread crumbs

Salt and black pepper to taste

Preparation:

Mix ground beef with garlic, onion, salt, pepper, and bread crumbs.

Divide beef into 2 halves; put ½ in a baking dish.

Peel and cut egg in ½ and put in the middle; add carrot, potato, and tomato sauce. Cover with the other ½ of beef.

Sprinkle the top with bread crumbs and bake at 350°F for 40 minutes.

Serve hot with vegetables.

Picadillo

Serves 4 to 6

Ingredients:

½ pound bofe (cow or calf's lungs)

½ pound chopped pajarilla (cow's pancreas or inners)

½ pound chopped heart

1 chopped small onion

1 minced garlic clove

1 chopped small tomato

2 tablespoons canola oil

1 cup water

3 chopped sweet peppers

Salt and pepper to taste

Sofrito (see recipe on page 86)

Preparation:

Clean bofe, pajarilla, and heart; cut them into small pieces.

Season with garlic, onion, salt, and pepper.

Heat oil in a skillet and lightly fry already seasoned pieces of bofe, parjarilla, and heart.

Add the rest of ingredients; cover and simmer until tender.

Serve hot with your starch of preference and hot sauce (optional).

Tongue in Sauce
(Lengua en salsa)

Serves 4 to 6

Ingredients:

1 beef tongue

2 chopped tomatoes

1 chopped onion

1 chopped large green bell pepper

2 minced garlic cloves

2 tablespoons tomato paste

Salt and black pepper to taste

Preparation:

Wash tongue thoroughly.

Fill a large pot ½ full of water and boil tongue 3 to 4 hours (add more water if necessary). Let cool.

Peel off the membrane of tongue and slice into ½ -inch thick pieces.

Put tongue in a casserole with a cup of water and add the rest of ingredients.

Cook over low heat until tongue is soft and sauce has thickened.

Tongue in Wine Sauce

(Lengua al vino)

Serves 4 to 6

Ingredients:

1 beef tongue

¼ cup canola oil

1 cup chopped onions

5 minced garlic cloves

½ cup chopped green peppers

2 ½ cups red wine

1 cup beef broth

¼ cup vinegar

½ teaspoon ground pepper

2 teaspoons salt

Preparation:

Wash tongue thoroughly.

Fill a large pot ½ full of water and boil tongue 3 to 4 hours (add more water if necessary). Let cool.

Remove tongue and take off the thick top layer. Trim any fat and cut into thin slices.

In a separate pan, heat oil and fry green pepper, garlic, and onion.

Add wine, beef broth, vinegar, pepper, and salt.

Add tongue slices to mix and cook slowly until tender.

Liver and Onions
(Hígado encebollado)

Serves 4

Ingredients:

2 pounds beef liver steaks

4 sliced large onions

Salt and black pepper to taste

Canola oil

Preparation:

Wash and remove white film from liver; season to taste with salt and pepper.

Heat oil in a skillet and brown liver two at a time on both sides. Remove liver.

Cook half portion of sliced onions until transparent, then add some more oil and cook remaining onions.

Remove onions and transfer liver steaks to the skillet; add half portion of onions to liver and heat for 1 minute. Reserve the other half portion of onions.

Serve liver and place reserved half portion of cooked onions over liver.

Bofe

Serves 4 to 6

Ingredients:

1 pound bofe (cow or calf's lungs)

1 chopped medium onion

1 minced garlic clove

1 chopped small tomato

Salt and pepper to taste

Canola oil (for frying)

Preparation:

Cut bofe in medium size strips; season to taste with salt and pepper.

Deep-fry bofe until brown and drain on paper towels.

In another skillet, add some oil and lightly fry onion and garlic.

Add tomato to onion and garlic and cook for 5 minutes.

Serve mix on the side or pour over bofe.

Pork Rinds
(Chicharrones)

Serves 4 to 6

Ingredients:

4 pounds pork skin (with fat)

½ cup water

Canola oil (for frying)

Salt and pepper to taste

Preparation:

Cut pork skin into bite-size pieces; season to taste with salt and pepper.

Put pork skin pieces in a large skillet and add water.

Cover and cook on low until water is consumed and pieces start to fry.

Continue to fry in hot oil until brown and crispy; drain on paper towels.

Pork Ribs in Chipotle Sauce

(Costillas de puerco con salsa chipotle)

Serves 6

Ingredients:

3 pounds pork ribs

4 ½ cups honey chipotle barbecue sauce

½ cup water

Preparation:

Preheat oven to 350°F. Cut ribs into serving size portions and place in a 13 x 9 x 2-inch aluminum baking pan.

Marinate in 3 cups of sauce and water for 35 minutes.

Cover with aluminum foil and cook for 2 ½ hours.

Brush remaining sauce over ribs and cook for 35 additional minutes.

NOTE: Sweet Baby Ray's Gourmet Sauces is one of Nilsa's favorites. If you use this brand you will need about 2 squeezable bottles (18 ounces each). It can be bought at supermarkets.

Iguana Adobada

Serves 4 to 6

Ingredients:

1 iguana

3 minced garlic cloves

4 chopped culantro leaves

4 chopped green or red peppers

1 chopped medium onion

4 diced pear tomatoes

¼ teaspoon oregano

¼ cup annatto oil

Salt and black pepper to taste

1½ tablespoons canola oil

10 cups water

Preparation:

Take off iguana's head, and hang iguana to let blood drain out.

Meanwhile boil water in a large pot; add salt and iguana. Let boil for 45 minutes.

Remove iguana from the stove and let cool.

Skin and dismember iguana by cutting it down the spine, dividing the halves into three pieces and the legs into two.

Heat oil in a large skillet and lightly fry iguana.

Add the rest of ingredients and cook on low until iguana is tender.

Iguana Stew

(Iguana guisada)

Serves 4 to 6

Ingredients:

1 gravid female iguana

Hot red pepper and garlic to taste

Salt to taste

1-2 chili peppers

Coconut oil

Water

Preparation:

Skin iguana, removing the insides and saving the eggs, including the yellow ones, heart, and liver.

Dismember iguana by cutting it down the spine, dividing the halves into three pieces and the legs in two.

Heat coconut oil in large skillet and brown iguana lightly. Add hot pepper and garlic to taste; brown a little longer.

Boil eggs in their shells with chili pepper for 30 minutes; peel eggs.

Dice liver and heart.

In a large pot, add 1½ cup of water, salt to taste, boiled eggs, liver, heart, and yellow eggs to meat.

Cook until broth has all but disappeared.

Serve with rice and beans.

CULTURAL NOTE: *This iguana stew is a native recipe of the Emberá-Wounaan Indians, Darien Province. They run out and catch themselves a gravid female iguana. They usually boil the iguana eggs for 10 minutes and then sun-dry them. This method of cooking the eggs adds a very unique flavor; a cheese-like flavor, according to some people. People from Darien enjoy them tremendously!*

Rabbit

(Conejo pintao')

Serves 6 to 8

Ingredients:

1 rabbit

4 cups brine water

3 garlic cloves

Salt to taste

Canola oil (for frying)

Preparation:

Cut up meat into long strips and discard bones.

To remove some of the strong wild flavor, soak meat for 1 hour in brine water, containing 1 tablespoon of salt per quart. Drain strips of meat.

Mash garlic cloves and rub on meat and season to taste with salt.

Dry strips out in the sun or hang them over a fogón or a rustic stove. (Note: meat can also be dried in a smoker).

Cut the strips into 3-inch pieces and deep-fry rabbit.

Serve with white rice and your favorite salad

Rabbit Stew

Serves 6

Ingredients:

2 pounds rabbit

1 large onion

½ teaspoon oregano

2 bay leaves

2 tablespoons tomato sauce

2 minced garlic cloves

1 lemon

1 cinnamon stick

¼ cup olive oil

Salt and pepper to taste

Preparation:

Store-bought rabbits are usually cut up. If not, separate the parts of rabbit with a butcher knife at home.

Wash rabbit with water and lemon.

Heat oil in a skillet and brown rabbit; season with salt, pepper, oregano, and garlic.

Cook rabbit until lightly browned. Remove and set aside.

Cut onion into rings and place in the same skillet you used before; add bay leaves and tomato sauce. Cook and stir for 5 minutes.

Add rabbit and cinnamon stick; cook on low for 50 minutes, or until rabbit is fully cooked.

CULTURAL NOTE: *Panamanians use store-bought farmed rabbits or wild rabbits that they got themselves. Rabbit meat is often compared to chicken because of its flavor and easy preparation. In fact, it is said that rabbit and chicken can be used in the same type of dishes. These rabbit recipes belong to Ofelina Lasso (Nilsa's mother). The first recipe is an easy recipe. First, you must cut up all the meat and discard the bones. You can rob garlic on the meat and season with salt. Dry meat out in the sun (for about a day) or hang pieces of meat over a fogón (rustic stove) or smoker. Drying and frying the rabbit is the most traditional way of cooking it in the rural areas of Panama. The second recipe (Rabbit Stew) appears to be the most common way of preparing rabbit in the city. Some people usually braise the parts of the rabbit beforehand, and then make a stew with them.*

BREADS

Breads have a direct connection with the European and U.S. presence in Panama. This is evident across Panama where a quick breakfast may be *hojaldras/hojaldres*, *micha* or *flauta* bread with white cheese, accompanied by a cup of *café con leche* (coffee with milk or creamer) or black coffee. Not too long ago, it was almost a ritual to go to the local bakery and buy freshly made *micha, flauta, pan de bolitas* and *moña bread*. In recent years, this custom has been fading away rapidly in urban areas because of the increasing popularity of cold cereals and loaf breads which are available at local grocery stores and major supermarkets.

Panamanian Micha Bread
(Pan micha)

Serves (varies)

Ingredients:

6 cups flour

1 pack yeast

¼ cup lukewarm water

2 cups warm milk

2 tablespoons melted butter

2 tablespoons sugar

2 teaspoons salt

Preparation:

In a bowl, dissolve yeast with 1 teaspoon sugar and lukewarm water. Let it stand for 5 minutes.

Add salt, butter, 2 tablespoons sugar, and warm milk.

Mix 3 cups of flour very well, then add the rest slowly.

Sprinkle flour liberally onto a cutting board or a table; place dough and knead until it becomes smooth and elastic.

Grease a large glass bowl and make a ball out of dough; place it in the bowl rolling it around in grease.

Cover dough with a damp cloth and let it rise for 2 ½, or until double in size.

Press dough down and let it stand for 30 minutes, or until double in size

Lightly grease 2 pans. Divide dough into oval-shaped rolls, place in pan and let rise for 15 additional minutes.

Bake at 350°F 35 for 40 minutes, or until golden brown.

CULTURAL NOTE: During our research we confirmed that the French passed on the micha bread recipe to Panamanians. In the 1800s, the French came to Panama to build the Canal. While in Panama, the French missed many things about their country, one of them was their traditional large loaf of bread, known as "miche." Soon enough, this delicious bread became one of Panama's favorites. Panamanians couldn't pronounce the word "miche" correctly and it became "pan micha." Today, "miche" or "micha" is one of the most popular breads across the nation.

TIPS: the dough can be prepared in a bread machine, but don't over knead.

Egg Bread
(Rosca de huevo)

Serves (varies)

Ingredients:

3 cups flour

1 pack yeast

1 dozen egg yolks

4 tablespoons water

1 cup mixed warm milk and lukewarm water (½ and ½)

3 tablespoons melted butter

1 tablespoon sugar

1 tablespoon salt

1 egg (optional)

Preparation:

In a bowl, dissolve yeast, sugar, and salt in mixed warm milk and lukewarm water. Set aside.

Beat yolks, adding 4 tablespoons of water, then strain mix.

Sift flour in a bowl and empty the bowl onto a table or a board.

Make a large hole in the middle of flour and pour in all ingredients.

Mix well and knead until dough makes dimples when being cut.

Hand shape dough into a rope or braid; join at the ends to create an oval (which is the traditional shape).

Bake at 350°F for 30 minutes, or until golden brown. It can be brushed with a beaten egg 5 minutes before removing from the oven.

CULTURAL NOTE: This Egg Bread, also known as Christmas Bread or Rosca Navideña, is traditionally eaten during the Christmas holidays in Panama. It is what the Jews called Challah bread, which is an important part of their tradition. It became a Panamanian tradition and it's extremely popular at Christmas. It's absolutely mouth-watering!

Hojaldres or Hojaldas

Serves 6 to 8

Ingredients:

1 pound flour

2 tablespoons baking powder

1 cup warm water

2 eggs

Dash salt

1 tablespoon canola oil

Preparation:

In a large mixing bowl, mix flour, baking powder, and salt.

Add eggs and water. Mix well. The dough will be sticky at first.

Sprinkle some flour while kneading.

Lightly grease a large glass bowl and make a ball out of dough; place it in the bowl rolling it around in grease until smooth.

Cover the bowl with a kitchen towel or plastic wrap. Let stand for 2 hours.

Heat oil in a large skillet. Pull off 2 to 3-inch pieces of dough. Make small balls and stretch each ball as you drop it into the oil.

Deep-fry hojaldres until lightly golden; drain on paper towels. Serve warm for breakfast.

CULTURAL NOTE: *Panamanians love this dish. They call it hojaldres, hojaldras (ojaldas) or arepas de harina. Although, it can be eaten as a little bite, it is usually served for breakfast. It's very popular across the nation! Hojaldres are made of wheat-flour, an important European and American ingredient passed on to Panamanian culture. Sometimes, people sprinkle powdered sugar over it. American visitors call it the Panamanian doughnut or fried bread. Nilsa's husband, who is an American, loves them with honey.*

TIPS: *Best if dough is prepared the night before, saved and covered in a plastic container or a glass bowl, and refrigerated until the next day.*

Doughnuts

(Bueñuelos de viento)

Serves 8 to 10

Ingredients:

3 cups All-purpose flour

1 tablespoon grated lemon rind

½ teaspoon butter

½ teaspoon salt

4 beaten eggs

1 teaspoon baking powder

¼ cup powdered sugar

2 cups water

Canola oil (for frying)

Preparation:

Bring water and butter to a boil. Remove from heat.

Slowly add flour, salt, and baking powder, beating vigorously with a wooden spoon, until all flour is used up.

Slowly, add beaten eggs, mixing until batter thickens.

Drop teaspoonfuls of batter in hot oil. Try to give them a round shape. Remove with a slotted spoon when golden brown.

Drain on paper towels and lightly sprinkle powdered sugar over the top. Serve hot!

Coconut Bread

(Pan de coco)

Serves (varies)

Ingredients:

9 cups flour

14 ½ teaspoons baking powder

2 teaspoons baking soda

½ pound raisins

2 pounds grated coconut

3 melted margarine sticks

4 cups sugar

2 teaspoons salt

1 teaspoon ground clove

2 teaspoons cinnamon powder

2 teaspoons nutmeg

3 cups evaporated milk

3 cups water

Preparation:

Mix all ingredients together.

Grease and flour molds and fill molds 2/3 with dough.

Bake at 350°F until done.

Banana Nut Bread

(Pan de guineo y nueces)

Serves (varies)

Ingredients:

1 cup mashed ripe banana

½ cup chopped walnuts

1/3 cup vegetable shortening (or margarine)

½ cup sugar

2 eggs

1¾ cups sifted flour

1 teaspoon baking powder

½ teaspoon salt

Preparation:

Mix together shortening (or margarine) and sugar.

Add eggs, mix well.

Sift together dry ingredients; add small portions of mashed banana, mixing well after each addition.

Add nuts and mix well. Pour into a well-greased 9 x 5 x 3-inch loaf pan.

Bake at 350°F for 45 minutes, or until done.

Remove from pan. Let cool and serve or store.

Perfect Corn Bread

(Pan de maíz)

Serves 6 to 8

Ingredients:

2 cups flour

¼ cup sugar

4 teaspoons baking powder

¾ teaspoon salt

1 cup yellow corn meal

2 eggs

1 cup evaporated milk

¼ cup margarine

Preparation:

Sift flour with sugar, baking powder, and salt.

Stir in corn meal.

Add eggs, milk and margarine. Beat with electric beater until smooth.

Put in a greased 9 x 9 x 2-inch bread mold.

Bake 425°F for 25 minutes.

Ginger Bread
(Pan de jengibre)

Serves 6

Ingredients:

1½ cups flour

½ cup margarine

1 egg

¾ teaspoon salt

¾ teaspoon baking soda

½ teaspoon cinnamon powder

½ cup sugar

½ cup light cane syrup

¾ teaspoon ground ginger

½ cup boiling water

Preparation:

Mix margarine and sugar until creamy; add egg and cane syrup.

Sift together dry ingredients and add to mixture.

Add small volumes of water to mixture, beating after each addition.

Bake in a greased and lightly floured 8 x 8 x 2-inch bread mold at 350°F for 35 minutes.

Afro-Panamanian-Style Hot Cross Buns

Serves 18

Ingredients:

3½ cups flour

4½ teaspoons dry yeast

1 teaspoon cinnamon powder

¾ cup milk

½ cup canola oil

¼ cup sugar

¾ teaspoon salt

3 eggs

½ cup dried currants

1 cup crystallized fruit

1 egg white

Ingredients for frosting:

1½ cups powdered sugar

1 egg white

¼ teaspoon pure vanilla extract

Dash salt

Milk, if needed

Preparation:

Mix 2 cups of flour, yeast, and cinnamon in a large mixing bowl.

Warm milk, canola oil, sugar, and salt; add to dry mixture.

Add 3 eggs and beat with an electric mixer on medium speed for 3 minutes, or until mixture is smooth.

Add currants and remaining flour to make soft dough.

Shape into a ball and place in a lightly greased bowl, turning once.

Cover and let rise in warm place for about 1½ hours.

Punch down, turn out on floured surface; cover and let stand for 10 minutes.

Divide into 18 pieces and form into smooth balls.

Place them on greased baking sheet 2 inches apart.

Cover and let rise for 35 minutes, or until double in size.

Cut shallow cross in each and brush top with slightly beaten egg white. Reserve some egg white.

Bake at 350°F 15 to 18 minutes.

Preparation for Frosting:

Mix 1½ cups powdered sugar with reserved egg white (use another egg white, if necessary), ¼ teaspoon pure vanilla extract and a dash of salt. Add milk, if needed.

Cool and lightly frost buns with this mixture.

Zucchini Bread
(Pan de zucchini)

Serves 10 to 12

Ingredients:

3 cups grated zucchini

8 ounces fresh pineapple chunks

3 cups flour

2 cups sugar

3 eggs

1¼ cups canola oil

2 teaspoons vanilla

1 teaspoon baking powder

1 teaspoon baking soda

½ teaspoon allspice

3 teaspoons cinnamon powder

½ teaspoon nutmeg

¼ teaspoon clove

1 cup walnut

Dash salt

Preparation:

Beat sugar, oil, and vanilla with an electric mixer on medium speed for 5 minutes.

Add eggs one at a time, while mixing on low speed.

Mix with grated zucchini and pineapple chunks.

Combine flour, baking powder, baking soda, salt, nuts, and spices.

Combine everything and mix well.

Place dough in two greased 8 x 4-inch baking pans.

Bake at 390°F for 60 minutes, or until done.

CULTURAL NOTE: Coconut bread, banana nut bread, perfect corn bread, ginger bread, hot cross buns, and zucchini breads are really European, Caribbean, or indigenous recipes that Afro-Panamanians have incorporated to their gastronomy. Of course, they have given these recipes their own touch. We collected most of the above Afro-Panamanian bread recipes during our trip across Panama.

Bon Bread

Serves (makes 3 loaves)
Ingredients:
3-4 cups flour
1 pack granulated yeast
2 tablespoons sugar
¼ cup lukewarm skim milk
½ cup brown sugar
½ teaspoon salt
½ teaspoon ground allspice
2 tablespoons soft margarine or butter
1 teaspoon cinnamon
½ teaspoon nutmeg
½ teaspoon ground ginger
¼ teaspoon ground cloves
½ teaspoon dried ground orange peel
1 butter stick
1 teaspoon vanilla
½ cup molasses
1 cup raisins
1 cup chopped candied fruit
1 beaten egg
1 tablespoon molasses

Preparation:

Dissolve yeast with 1 tablespoon of sugar in lukewarm milk and let it get frothy.

In a separate bowl, place 3½ cups flour with remaining sugar, salt, and spices; mix well.

Add small pieces of butter to yeast mixture, stirring brown sugar, vanilla, and ½ cup of molasses; mix with an electric mixer on medium speed. Add mixture to flour mix.

Stir in raisins and candied fruit to mix.

Remove from bowl and knead on a surface with some flour for 5 minutes, or until smooth. If too sticky, add remaining flour.

Place dough in a greased bowl, cover and let rise until double in size. Remove the air punching a fist into dough. Divide into three to create three dough balls.

Place on a greased tray, cover and let rise until double in size again.

Bake at 350°F for 20 minutes.

Mix egg and 1 tablespoon molasses with a manual mixer; brush the surface of loaves and bake for 15 additional minutes.

CULTURAL NOTE: Marino Jaén Espinosa in his article about the history of bon or bun, reports: "The bun is a semi-sweet bread sprinkled with raisins and other fruits and spices such as vanilla and cinnamon. This tradition originated in England, but was brought to the Antilles during colonial times. The black slaves brought forcibly from Africa picked it up and incorporated the bun to their gastronomy. The bun arrived to Panama in the late 1800s during the French Canal project. Many of the workers for this project came from Jamaica and other Caribbean islands, so the bun traveled with them. Then, between 1904 and 1914 during the completion of the canal by the U.S. government, another big group of black Caribbean immigrants came to Panama, mainly from Barbados. Today, Panamanians from every ethnic background enjoy the bun. It has even become a common dish for Holy Week, since it has been said that it represents the bread distributed by Jesus during the Last Supper." There are somewhat different bon recipes but the concept and cultural meaning are essentially the same. The bon recipe included in this book belongs to Catherine Rogers (Jiwanda's grandmother) who was a Panamanian of Afro-Caribbean descent. Some Panamanians prepare their bon at home. Others buy it from street vendors or at local bakeries. Bon bread can also be found at places called bones. This bread is usually served with yellow cheese, butter, a glass of milk, a cup of hot tea or a cold beverage.

Yaniqueque

Serves (varies)

Ingredients:

5 pounds All-purpose flour

3 cups fresh coconut milk or evaporated milk

2 butter sticks

4 tablespoons lard

3 teaspoons baking powder

3 tablespoons sugar

1 teaspoon salt

Preparation:

Mix all ingredients; add milk last in small amounts.

Knead dough for about 15 minutes, or until smooth.

Pull pieces of dough to make small rolls. Let rise for 1 to 2 hours.

Bake at 350°F for 25 minutes, or until lightly browned.

CUTURAL NOTE: *Yaniqueque is a typical recipe from the province of Bocas del Toro where there is a strong Afro-Caribbean influence. While researching, we found out that, in the Dominican Republic, a yaniqueque (or Dominican Johny's cake) is a fried tortilla made of wheat flour, egg whites, salt, and water. It is considered a comfort food, usually sold at food stands along the beaches of this beautiful Caribbean island. The Panamanian yaniqueque is typically served as a dinner roll or snack. The ingredients and method of preparation differ a bit, since Afro-Panamanians do not add egg whites and they prefer to bake it.*

Journey Cake or Johnnycakes

Serves 8 to 12

Ingredients:

5 pounds flour

4 tablespoons baking powder

½ teaspoon dry yeast

Fresh coconut milk (of two coconuts)

½ pound butter

¼ pound vegetable shortening (like Crisco)

3 teaspoons sugar

6 teaspoons salt

2 tablespoons canola oil

Preparation:

Mix coconut milk, vegetable shortening, butter, salt, sugar, yeast, and baking powder until all ingredients are dissolved.

Add flour to coconut milk and knead for about 10 minutes.

Shape dough into a long loaf; cut into medium size pieces. Take each piece and sprinkle with flour and make little biscuit or cakes. Pinch them with a fork.

Grease a large skillet with oil and place cakes in a pan.

Cover and place the skillet in the coals in a barbecue grill or fire place. Cover and put coals or wood on top of the covered skillet.

Let journal cakes cook for 10 minutes, or until they start to smell like coconut.

CULTURAL NOTE: *This bread was originally called journey cake because it was usually taken by individuals when packing food for a long journey. People with a Caribbean accent changed the word "journey" to "johnny." Due to this linguistic variation, this bread became commonly known as johnnycakes. This bread is consumed by ex-slaves who settled along the Caribbean coast of Central America. It is also eaten in most Caribbean islands. Journey cakes or johnnycakes are one of Bocas del Toro's favorite breads.*

Bakes

Serves 4 to 6

Ingredients:

2 cups flour

2 teaspoons baking powder

1 cup water

2 teaspoon salt

¼ cup canola oil

Canola oil (for frying)

Preparation:

In a large mixing bowl, mix flour, baking powder, and salt.

Add oil and water; mix well.

Heat oil in a skillet and spoon dough in hot oil one at a time.

Brown on both sides, making sure the bakes are cooked all the way through.

Remove bakes and drain on paper towels.

CULTURAL NOTE: *This recipe is made by Afro-Panamanians. Bakes were brought to Panama by Jamaicans who came during the construction of the Panama Canal. The original style of this recipe used to be made by Catherine Gale (Jiwanda's grandmother). A variation of this recipe (from Jamaica) calls for a thicker dough which is kneaded and cut into rounds. Then, these rounds are flattened and fried. Jiwanda enjoys bakes with cheese or jam.*

DESSERTS
AND
SWEETS

Rural Panama offers several traditional homemade sweets. The most popular desserts across the countryside are *huevitos de leche*, *dulce de leche*, *cocada*, Panamanian meringue, *cabanga* (a very unique dish made of green papaya, coconut, and cane syrup), *bienmesabe chiricano* (made with fresh raw milk, rice, raspadura, and spices), *suspiros*, *suripico*, *clarita*, *rosquitos/as*, and *queque*. Other quite popular desserts are rice pudding, *mazamorra*, cashew fruit marmalade, fruit cake, sweetened bean pie and candied pumpkin squash. The fruit cake, bean pie and candied pumpkin are usually served during the holidays and special celebrations, for example, Christmas, New Year's Eve, and Holy Week. Another dessert is *mamallena* (bread pudding) which is well-liked across the nation. A variety of sweets and baked desserts are prepared in rural areas as well as in other parts of the country, such as cake, pie, *sopa borracha* (sponge cake soaked in syrup and rum or brandy), *sopa de gloria*, *bocado del Rey*, *bocado de la Reina*, *arroz con cacao*, and many others included in this section. In Panama, it is a tradition to give desserts as presents during Holy week and Christmas.

Mazamorra

Serves 10 to 12

Ingredients:

15 fresh corn on the cob

4 cups *nance*

1 grated coconut (optional)

1 pound fresh white pressed cheese

1 teaspoon salt

2 cups sugar

4 cups warm water

Preparation:

Remove corn kernels and put in the blender with 2 cups of warm water; mix well. Strain to obtain only the juice of the corn (repeat process, if necessary).

Do the same with coconut and the rest of warm water.

Extract nance pulp by squeezing; discard nance seeds.

Mix corn juice, coconut milk, nance pulp, salt, and sugar; mix well.

Pour in a pan and cook over medium-low heat for 35 minutes, or until it thickens. Stir frequently with a wooden spoon.

Pour in cups and serve hot or cold. Crumble cheese on top.

CULTURAL NOTE: *Panamanians prepare two similar mazamorra recipes: Pesada and mazamorra. Pesada is prepared with flour, while mazamorra is made with fresh corn. The method of preparation and other ingredients are basically the same. In some regions, people like to add grated coconut to mazamorra.*

Suripico

Serves 6 to 8

Ingredients:

8 cups milk (fresh raw milk is preferred)

1 cinnamon stick (optional)

6-8 cups sugar

Preparation:

Pour milk and cinnamon in a large thick pot.

Mix, while adding sugar. With a wooden spoon, stir until sugar is dissolved and mixture is boiling.

Reduce heat and let cook slowly. It is ready when mixture is very lumpy.

Serve hot or cold.

CULTURAL NOTE: This is the original recipe of the Gutiérrez family from Bayano and Chepo, province of Panama. They cook suripico on a fogón, a cooking area or a rustic stove, usually made of bricks or stones. However, it can be cooked on a stove top on low heat.

Queques

Serves 16 to 20

Ingredients:

1 pound flour

½ pound grated coconut

1-2 cups honey

1 ½ teaspoons salt

½ teaspoon cinnamon powder

1 teaspoon baking soda

2-3 tablespoons shortening

Preaparation:

Heat the oven to 350°F.

Mix all dry ingredients.

Add shortening and honey; mix well.

Knead dough and form into balls of the size of your preference.

Place balls of dough onto a greased cookie sheet, leaving enough room for expansion.

Press into cookie shapes and bake for 30 minutes.

Mamallena

Serves (varies)

Ingredients:

12 slices white bread

2 cups milk

4 eggs

1 cup sugar

¼ pound melted butter

¼ teaspoon salt

1 teaspoon pure vanilla extract

½ cup raisins

Preparation:

Place bread in a mixing bowl and add milk. Let it sit 20 to 25 minutes.

Tear bread into small pieces with hands.

Add sugar and mix well.

Beat eggs lightly and add to bread.

Add remaining ingredients and pour into a greased baking pan.

Bake at 350°F for about 1 hour, or until it is dry and lightly browned.

Let cool and serve.

Peach Palm Fruit Flan
(Flan de pixbae)

Serves (varies)

Ingredients:

4 cups peeled and chopped peach palm fruit

4 cups milk

3 cups sugar

4 eggs

3 egg yolks

1 teaspoon pure vanilla extract

2 cups whipped cream

3 tablespoons water

Preparation:

In a pan cook sugar and water over a medium heat until caramel colored.

Pour caramel in a 9 x 12 round pan.

Place peach palm fruit with milk in a blender and blend until mixture is fine. Pass through a strainer.

Beat eggs lightly with yolks; add mixture.

Add vanilla extract and whipped cream.

Pour in pan; preheat oven to 350ºF and bake inside a double larger mold with water. Try the center to see if it is dry.

Cool and serve.

Yuca Pone
(Enyucado)

Serves 6 to 8

Ingredients:

1 grated coconut

3 pounds grated yuca

1 cup raisin

4 cups tightly packed brown sugar

4 tablespoons cinnamon

Dash salt

2 tablespoons margarine or butter

2 teaspoons vanilla

3 cups water

Preparation:

Add water to grated coconut; mix and squeeze milk out and strain.

Pour coconut milk in a bowl and add yuca and the rest of ingredients, except butter; mix well.

Place mixture in an 8 x 10-inch greased pan. Top with pieces of butter and sprinkle with cinnamon.

Bake in oven at 350°F for about 1 ½ hours, or when top is dry and lightly browned.

CULTURAL NOTE: This is an *Afro-Caribbean-style enyucado and it is very popular in the Afro-Caribbean communities of Panama City, Colon, and Bocas del Toro.*

Yuca Pudding

(Enyucado)

Serves 6 to 8

Ingredients:

1 grated coconut

3 pounds grated yuca

4 cups sugar

2 tablespoons butter

2 tablespoons grained anise

Preparation:

Add water to grated coconut; mix and squeeze milk out and strain.

Pour coconut milk in a bowl and add yuca and the rest of ingredients, except butter; mix well.

Place mixture in a 9 x 9-inch greased pan and top with pieces of butter.

Bake in oven at 350°F for about 1 ½ hours.

CULTURAL NOTE: *This is a country-style enyucado and it is commonly prepared in the rural regions of Panama.*

Enyucado

Serves 8 to10

Ingredients:

3 pounds yuca root

4-5 cups cane syrup

Preparation:

Peel and cut yuca into 2-inch chunks.

In a large pot, simmer cane syrup and yuca over medium-low heat for 40 to 45 minutes, or until soft.

Serve warm and enjoy its unique flavor!

CULTURAL NOTE: This enyucado is the original recipe of Arquímedes Gutiérrez (Nilsa's father). He had a large farm in the Chepo-Bayano area. He used to make this delicious enyucado recipe at special gatherings or parties with relatives, friends, and workers. This was a yearly event, when the sugar cane was ready to be harvested. It was a lot fun!

Mary Jane Cookies

Serves 24

Ingredients:

2 ½ cups tightly packed light brown sugar

1 ¼ cup shortening (Crisco- butter flavor)

4 cups All-purpose flour

3 eggs

1 cup ground and tightly packed crystallized fruit

1 cup ground and tightly packed raisins

2 teaspoons vanilla

1/3 cup water

1 teaspoon salt

1 teaspoon baking soda

Preparation:

Beat sugar and shortening with an electric mixer on low to medium speed until creamy; add eggs and continue to mix.

Add vanilla, water, fruits, and raisins.

Mix, while adding flour, until all ingredients are combined.

Spoon cookie batter onto non-stick cookie sheet.

Bake at 350°F for 20 minutes, or until browned; do not burn.

CULTURAL NOTE: *Mary Jane cookies are well-known among residents and non-residents of the former Canal Zone area. These cookies were usually purchased at the Commissaries, where only the Zonians had buying privileges.*

Candied Pumpkin Squash
(Dulce de zapallo)

Serves (varies)

Ingredients:

2 cups cubed pumpkin squash

1 cup cane syrup (or to taste)

1 cup coconut milk

1 cinnamon stick

Preparation:

Cook all ingredients in a saucepan, stirring constantly.

Candied pumpkin squash is ready when mixture begins to separate from the bottom of the pan.

Serve warm.

Red Bean Pie
(Dulce de frijoles)

Serves (varies)

Ingredients:

1 ½ pound red beans

½ pound sifted flour

2 cups cane syrup

1 ½ cups evaporated milk

1 cup grated coconut (optional)

1 tablespoon cinnamon powder

¼ teaspoon salt

Preparation:

Soak and wash beans very well. Put beans in a large pot with 4 quarts of water; cover and cook until soft.

Grind or blend beans in a blender or a food processor.

Strain, adding small volumes of water; reserve juice and discard the rest.

Dissolve flour in warm water until a creamy batter is formed.

Mix reserved juice, cinnamon powder, milk, and cane syrup; cook at low temperature for about 1 hour.

Add creamy batter and keep cooking at low temperature until it thickens; stir constantly.

It's ready when smooth and brown with a pie-like consistency.

Top with grated coconut if desired and serve.

CULTURAL NOTE: *Red bean pie is a traditional recipe, especially in the rural areas of Panama. This recipe is the original recipe of Juanita Begambre Lasso (Nilsa's grandmother). It was customary to make this pie during Holy Week. Today, this is a tradition that seems to be fading away.*

Sopa Borracha

(Sponge cake soaked in syrup, rum and whisky or brandy)

Serves (varies)

Ingredients for cake:

3 cups flour

2 teaspoons baking powder

4 eggs

¼ teaspoon salt

¼ stick butter

1 cup sugar

1 cup milk

1 teaspoon pure vanilla extract

Ingredients for syrup:

4 ½ cups sugar

4 cloves

3 cinnamon sticks

6 cups water

1 lime peel

1 cup raisins

2 cups prunes

1 cup rum

1 cup brandy or whisky

1 cup small silver candy balls (garnish)

Preparing Cake:

Mix flour, baking powder, and salt.

Grease a 12-inch jelly roll pan and dust with flour.

Preheat the oven at 350°F.

Mix butter and sugar with an electric mixer on medium speed until mixture is creamy; add eggs one at a time, while mixing.

Slowly add dry ingredients, while mixing; add milk and vanilla.

Pour mixture in pan and bake for about 20 minutes.

Cool and cut into 1-inch pieces.

Preparing Syrup:

Put sugar, water, cloves, lime peel, and cinnamon in a pot. When it caramelizes, remove lime peel, cloves, and cinnamon sticks.

Add raisins and prunes; let cook for a few minutes.

Cool and add rum and whisky (or brandy).

In a large and deep glass bowl place a layer of cake pieces and pour some syrup, then another layer of cake pieces, then syrup. Repeat the process until all cake pieces and syrup are used up.

Decorate top with small silver candy balls. Serve in small 4-ounce glass cups.

Sopa de Gloria

Serves (varies)
Ingredients:
6 eggs
1 ½ cups sugar
1 cup All-purpose flour
2 teaspoons baking powder
½ cup warm milk
¼ teaspoon salt
1 teaspoon almond extract

Ingredients for syrup:
3 cups sugar
3 cups water
1 teaspoon lemon juice

Ingredients for Cream:
1 can (14 ounces) condensed milk
2 cans (12 ounces) evaporated milk
1 cup water
4 egg yolks
1 cup chopped almonds
1 teaspoon almond extract
1 cup small silver candy balls (garnish)

Preparation:

Preheat oven to 350°F; cover baking tray with wax paper.

Separate egg yolks from egg whites. Beat egg yolks, add ½ cup sugar and keep mixing. Beat egg whites until thick and slowly add remaining sugar.

Put in all dry ingredients; add salt and almond extract to yolk mixture.

Slowly add egg white mixture and milk, as you stir.

Lightly grease the tray and cover with flour.

Pour in mixture and bake for about 20 minutes. Let cool and flip onto a cutting board.

Cut into shaped pieces and place in a deep pan or tray.

Preparing syrup: Heat these ingredients in a pot until they become syrup. Let cool and pour syrup over cake.

Preparing cream: Put all ingredients in a double boiler; stir slowly until creamy. Let cool.

Pour cream over cake and garnish with ground cinnamon, silver candy balls and almonds.

Sopa de gloria is usually served in small glass cups.

Bocado de la Reina

Serves (varies)

Ingredients:

1 can (12 ounces) cream milk

1 can (12 ounces) condensed milk

1 teaspoon salt

1 egg yolk

4 tablespoons cornstarch

½ cup raisins

½ cup prunes

1 cinnamon stick

½ cup rum

2 cups sugar, plus 1 cup for cream

1 teaspoon vanilla

1 sponge cake

2 cups water

Preparation:

Cut cake into squares, placing in a deep dish.

Place 2 cups of sugar with 1 cup of water to boil with prunes, raisins, and cinnamon stick.

Simmer until raisins are puffed. Turn the flame off and let cool.

Stir in rum and add beaten egg yolk; bathe cake pieces.

Heat milk with ½ cup of water in a double boiler; add 1cup sugar and 1 teaspoon salt.

Dissolve cornstarch in ½ cup of water; add it to mixture in a rather thin stream, stirring constantly. Let cook for10 minutes.

Add vanilla and pour cream over cake.

Garnish with beaten egg white meringue, putting two tablespoons sugar to every egg white (optional).

Decorate with silver candy balls. Serve in small glass cups.

Bocado del Rey

Serves 14 to 16

Ingredients:

1 sheet sponge cake

4 tablespoons cornstarch

4 tablespoons bitter cocoa

1 teaspoon salt

1 cup prunes

2 cups water

¼ bottle rum

1 teaspoon vanilla

1 can (12 ounces) condensed milk

1 ½ cup raisins

2 cups sugar

Peaches (to taste)

Plums (to taste)

Cherries (for decoration)

Preparation:

Mix water, sugar, 1 cup raisins, prunes, and cinnamon; boil syrup until thick and let cool. Stir in rum.

Prepare cream with condensed milk, salt, vanilla, cornstarch, and cocoa; put in double boiler, stirring constantly. Cook for 10 minutes.

Cut sponge cake and place in a deep glass serving dish, then soak with syrup.

Put in sliced peaches, ½ cup raisins, and plums.

Cover with cream and decorate with raisins, cherries, and prunes. Sprinkle with nuts if desired.

CULTURAL NOTE: Sopa borracha, sopa de gloria, bocado de la Reina, and bocado del Rey are very popular in Panamanian weddings.

Alfajor

Serves 6 (about 2 cookies per person)

Ingredients:

2 ¼ cups flour

¼ cup butter

3 ½ tablespoons powdered sugar

Dulce de leche or milk caramel

Preparation:

Sift all dry ingredients together on a clean surface. Make a hole in the middle and add small pieces of butter.

Use hands to incorporate the ingredients to make dough with a sandy consistency. Then make a ball and refrigerate for 30 minutes.

Put dough ball between two pieces of wax paper and roll over with a rolling pin until it reaches its thickness (about 1/16 inch). Cut circles 2 ½ inches in diameter.

Place circles on a greased baking sheet. Bake at 375°F for 12 minutes until lightly browned.

Let cool; take two cookies and fill the center with *"dulce de leche."*

CULTURAL NOTE: *This recipe is believed to be of Arab origin. It was adopted by the people of Andalusia, Spain. The above recipe is based on the original one brought by Spanish colonizers to the Americas. There are many variations of this recipe throughout Latin America. In Panama, this dish is better known in the Azuero Peninsula. This comes as no surprise to us, because in this region one can find various imported Spanish Colonial recipes that have suffered very few changes.*

TIPS: *For flavor add coconut flakes to filling and sprinkle cookies with powdered sugar.*

Manjar Blanco

Serves 8

Ingredients:

1 liter whole milk plus 2 ½ cups

1 can evaporated milk

3 ½ cups white sugar

2 tablespoons vanilla

1 butter stick

Cinnamon stick to taste

Preparation:

In a thick large pot, add the milks, sugar, and vanilla. Cook on medium flame, stirring occasionally until mix starts to thicken.

Add cinnamon stick and continue to stir constantly to prevent mix from sticking. Stop stirring when caramel reaches desired thickness.

To test caramel, put a drop of caramel in cold water, if it forms a ball, caramel is ready. Remove from the fire, discard cinnamon stick and add butter.

Mix until completely incorporated.

Bienmesabe

Serves 8

Ingredients:

½ liter whole milk

2 cups cream of rice

4 raspaduras (panela) (like Goya)

3 cups evaporated milk

Sugar to taste

Salt to taste

Water

Preparation:

Heat water to dissolve raspadura; add evaporated milk.

In a separate bowl mix cream of rice and whole milk.

Put both mixes in a large pot; add salt and sugar to taste and cook, stirring constantly until mixture thickens.

Pour into a bowl and let cool before serving.

CULTURAL NOTE: *Bienmesabe literally means "good tasting dessert or it tastes good to me." This seems to be a very traditional dessert, mostly prepared in the province of*

Chiriqui. It is a tradition that appears to be fading. When referring to this dessert, Panamanian Chef Melissa De León, also known as the "Cooking Diva," says that the Bienmesabe Chiricano is a "Delicious Lost Dessert from Panama." Customarily, Panamanians serve it with homemade white cheese.

Cocada

Serves (varies)

Ingredients:

1 pound grated coconut

2 cups cane syrup

Preparation:

In medium pot, pour cane syrup and boil over medium heat until it thickens.

Add grated coconut and mix consistently for 10 minutes, until coconut absorbs all cane syrup.

Let cool and serve.

Cocada with Cashews

Serves (varies)

Ingredients:

1 grated coconut

1 cup cashews

4-5 cups cane syrup

1 cinnamon stick

Preparation:

In a medium pot, cook coconut, cane syrup, and cinnamon for 2 hours; stirring consistently.

Add cashews and mix until mixture does not stick to bottom of the pot.

Serve warm.

CULTURAL NOTE: *Roasting cashew nuts for eating or making desserts is a tradition for Lent and Holy Week in Panama. People collect the nuts during the summer and roast them outdoors on a rustic stove or a fogón.*

Cashew Fruit Marmalade

Serves (varies)

Ingredients:

40 cashew fruits

4 solid panela blocks

4 cinnamon sticks

2 cups water

Preparation:

Wash cashew fruit and remove cashew nuts; cut fruit into 1-inch squares.

In a pan, place squares, cinnamon sticks, and water. Cook over medium-low heat for 40 or 45 minutes, stirring sporadically with a wooden spoon.

Chop or grind panela blocks; add to cashew fruit and mix well.

Cook until syrup is thick and dark color.

Let cool, put in glass containers and refrigerate until ready to serve.

Garnish with unsalted roasted cashew nuts.

Cabanga

Serves 10 to 12

Ingredients:

1 coconut

1 green papaya

2 cups cane syrup

Preparation:

Grate coconut and papaya.

Put coconut, papaya, and cane syrup in a pan; mix well and bring to a boil, until you can see the bottom of the pan.

Remove from stove. Place on cutting board, stretch and cut into small rectangular pieces.

Cool and wrap each piece with dry corn husk. Tie them up and store at room temperature.

Panamanian Taffy
(Melcocha)

Serves 4 to 6 dozens

Ingredients:

1 cup water

2 cups sugar

4 tablespoons butter

½ teaspoon pure vanilla extract or mint or lemon zest

Red food coloring

Preparation:

In a heavy pan, mix water, butter, and sugar and cook over low heat. Stir consistently until sugar is dissolved. Increase heat and bring mixture to a boil.

Place a candy thermometer in the pan; continue stirring. Cook and stir constantly until mixture reaches 248°F. When candy has reached desired temperature, remove from heat; remove thermometer without scraping sides and bottom of pan, pour mixture onto a greased large platter.

When cool enough to handle, add drops of vanilla or mint or lemon zest, and food coloring.

Grease your hands with butter; take a small portion of candy and begin pulling. Use only the tips of your fingers to pull.

Candy should no longer feel sticky when it has been pulled enough.

Twist each pulled strip slightly and place on waxed paper. When all the candy is pulled, cut each strip into 1-inch pieces. Wrap each piece in waxed paper and twist ends.

CULTURAL NOTE: Melcocha or alfandoque is very popular in some countries of Latin America and Spain. The above recipe is a typical taffy candy recipe from Panama. Melcocha is a traditional and famous hand-pulled taffy candy in Baños, Ecuador. In Costa Rica, Mexico, and El Salvador, this candy is also very well-liked. The basic ingredient for this candy is the same (sugar, cane syrup or panela); however, ingredients may vary from country to country. For example: Panamanians may choose to flavor this candy with vanilla, mint, anise or lemon zest, while other countries may add peanuts, grated coconut, nuts, cinnamon, sesame seeds or other spices and flavorings.

Huevitos de Leche

Serves 6 to 8

Ingredients:

2 liters milk

2 pounds sugar

1 teaspoon salt

1 tablespoon vanilla extract

Colorful candy wrappers

Preparation:

Mix milk with sugar and salt; cook mix on medium heat in a large thick pot (non aluminum), stir constantly to prevent sticking and burning, until mix is thick.

Add vanilla and remove from heat, let cool enough to be handled with hands.

Scoop out teaspoons of caramel and make small egg-shaped balls. Wrap them with candy wrappers.

Place them in a tray or pack them in small plastic bags.

TIPS: For added flavor add coconut flakes to the mix.

Meringues

Serves 4

Ingredients:

2 egg whites

3/4 cup sugar

¼ teaspoon salt

¼ teaspoon cinnamon

Preparation:

Beat egg whites; add sugar little by little and continue to beat until egg whites are stiff peaks.

Use tablespoon or decorative point pastry bag. Extrude batter unto a cookie sheet covered with parchment paper.

Bake at 300°F until meringues are lightly browned.

Suspiros

Serves 8 to 10

Ingredients:

1 pound cassava starch (or yuca starch)

2 eggs

3/4 cup sugar

1 tablespoon lemon or lime zest

½ teaspoon cream of tartar

Preparation:

Sift cassava starch in a large bowl, open a hole in the middle and place the rest of ingredients in the center.

Mix ingredients with a wooden spoon until it turns into dough.

Take pieces of dough, kneading each piece in the palm of your hands and elongating dough in the shape of a pencil. Then roll dough into spiral.

Bake on a non-stick cookie sheet at 250°F until suspiros are lightly browned.

Mango Mousse

Serves 4

Ingredients:

4 cups pureed mango

1 cup sugar

4 egg yolks

1 teaspoon unflavored gelatine

½ cup water

1 teaspoon lime juice

2 cups whipped cream

Preparation:

Beat sugar and egg yolks until tickens.

Dissolve gelatine in water and heat in double boiler; add egg yolks and stir vigorously.

Add lime juice and mango purée.

Let cool for an hour and add whipped cream; mix well.

Place in glass bowls and refrigerate for about 6 hours.

CULTURAL NOTE: The French get credit for creating the mousse. The Webster's New International Dictionary defines mouse as foam. "In cookery, it is a frozen dessert of sweetened and flavored whipped cream or thin cream and gelatine, frozen without stirring; a similar unsweetened product, often containing cheese or vegetables, and used for salad. A gelatine dish made of a purée of meat or fish lightened with whipped cream." The French influence is evident in this dish. Panamanians are using European ingredients and old cooking methods, while adding their own unique tropical flavors.

TIPS: To make mango purée, peel, and cut mango into small pieces. Blend in blender or food processor until mango is pureed.

Rice Pudding
(Arroz con leche)

Serves 4

Ingredients:

1 cup rice

2 ½ cups water

1 cup milk

1 can (14 ounces) evaporated milk

1 can (12 ounces) condensed milk

¼ cup sugar

½ teaspoon salt

1 tablespoon vanilla extract

1 cinnamon stick

Cinnamon Powder

Raisins (optional)

Preparation:

Wash and drain rice; cook rice with 1 ½ cups of water and salt.

When rice is tender, add milks, 1 cup water, sugar, vanilla, raisins, and cinnamon.

Cook for 20 minutes on low, stirring constantly to prevent sticking and burning, until mixture is thick.

Remove from heat; let cool and refrigerate for 10 minutes.

Decorate with cinnamon powder and serve.

VARIATION: Rice pudding has many variations; this is one of Jiwanda's favorite desserts!

Rice Pudding Chiriqui-Style
(Arroz con leche chiricano)

Serves 4

Ingredients:

3 cups rice

4 liters milk

4 cans (12 ounces) evaporated milk

3 crushed raspadura (panela)

½ teaspoon salt

1 tablespoon vanilla extract

8 tablespoons cinnamon

1 box (15 ounces) raisins

Preparation:

Wash and drain rice.

Heat 2 liters of milk in a large pot, when it starts to boil, add 2 cans of evaporated milk and three cups of rice.

Cook on low, stirring constantly to prevent sticking and burning, until mix is thick and milk is consumed.

Add 2 cans of milk and continue to stir.

When rice is soft, add panela little by little and stir constantly, tasting for sweetness.

Add remaining milk, raisins, vanilla, cinnamon (leave 2 tablespoons for topping), and salt.

Cook some more on low, continue to stir until desired consistency.

Remove from heat and serve in individual dishes.

Sprinkle with cinnamon.

VARIATION: The use of raspadura (panela) is what gives this Rice Pudding the flavor of the countryside.

Rice Chocolate Pudding with Coconut Milk
(Arroz con cacao)

Serves 8

Ingredientes:

1 pound rice

1 cup sugar

1 fresh coconut

4 ¼ cups water

2 tablespoons cocoa

¼ teaspoon salt

½ teaspoon vanilla extract

Cinnamon to taste

Preparation:

Wash and soak rice for 2 hours; drain.

Grate coconut; add ¼ cup water and strain; reserve coconut milk.

Add 4 cups of water to coconut and strain again; cook rice in this coconut milk and add salt.

When rice is soft, add sugar, cocoa, vanilla, and cinnamon.

Cook on low, uncovered, 20 additional minutes, or until mix is creamy.

Remove from heat, let cool and refrigerate 10 minutes.

Serve with reserved coconut milk.

Cofio

Serves 8

Ingredients:

1 pound fresh corn kernels

Sugar to taste

Preparation:

Toast corn kernels in a large skillet. When corn is well-toasted, let cool.

Grind corn in a grinder or a food processor and add sugar to taste. Enjoy!

Rice with Raisins
(Arroz con pasitas)

Serves 6 to 8

Ingredients:

2 ½ cups rice

3 cups water

1 cup cane syrup or brown sugar

1 cup raisins

1 teaspoon cinnamon

¼ teaspoon cloves powder

1 teaspoon vanilla

Salt to taste

Preparation:

In a large pot heat raisins, cane syrup, vanilla, salt, cloves, and water. Boil for 5 minutes, stirring well.

Add rice; stir and cook on low for 20 minutes, or until rice is soft.

Serve hot.

Darien's Angel Hair
(Cabello de ángel)

Serves 8 to 10

Ingredients:

1 large green papaya

4-5 cups cane syrup

¼ cup water

4 cinnamon sticks

Preparation:

Cut both ends of papaya to get rid of milky liquids.

Peel and slice papaya into wedges, as thickly or as thinly as you like. Discard seeds.

In a medium pot, add water and cook papaya, cinnamon, and cane syrup. When papaya turns red, it's ready! Remove cinnamon sticks.

Corn Pudding

(Pudín de maíz)

Serves 6 to 8

Ingredients:

3 cups corn meal

2 ½ cups coconut milk

2 cups sugar

¾ cup All-purpose flour

2 tablespoons vanilla

2 teaspoons baking powder

1 cup dark raisins

1 ½ teaspoon salt

Nutmeg to taste

Preparation:

Cook corn meal and coconut milk over medium-low heat. When it's almost done, remove and set aside for about half an hour.

Add vanilla, sugar, cinnamon, raisins, flour, nutmeg, and baking powder; mix well.

Pour mixture into well-greased baking pan.

Bake at 350°F for about 40 to 45 minutes.

Serve warm.

Orange Flan
(Flan de naranja)

Serves 6

Ingredients:

The juice of 25 oranges

Water equal to amount of orange juice from the oranges

1 ½ cups raisins

1 teaspoon vanilla extract

1 tablespoon cornstarch

Sugar to taste

Cinnamon

Preparation:

In a large pot heat water, add cornstarch and orange juice little by little, stirring constantly to prevent mixture from sticking.

Add raisins and sugar. Continue stirring until mixture has thickened.

Pour flan into glass pan and refrigerate.

Sour Orange Candy
(Dulce de naranja agria)

Serves 6 to 8

Ingredients:

The peel of 12 oranges

6 yucas

3 ½ cups cane syrup

Cinnamon sticks

Allspice

Preparation:

Soak orange peels in water for 2 days.

Boil orange peels with cinnamon sticks for 15 minutes. Take peels out and grind them. Discard cinnamon sticks.

Peel and boil yuca until soft. Remove and mash yuca and orange peel.

Add cane syrup and allspice to taste; cook until mixture is creamy.

Claritas

Serves (varies)

Ingredients:

2 pounds fine bread crumbs

2 pounds sugar

¼ cup water

1 teaspoon ground clove

Preparation:

In a large pot, cook sugar and cloves and bring to a boil.

Add bread crumbs and lower the heat to medium, stir constantly until mixture separates from sides.

Pour mixture unto a wet baking pan. Let cool and cut into 2-inch squares; sprinkle with bread crumbs.

Rosquitos

Serves (varies)

Dough ingredients:

2 cups flour

¼ cup butter

3 tablespoons sugar

1 teaspoon salt

½ cup water

Glaze ingredients:

2 cups sugar

2 cups water

1 drop red food coloring

Dough preparation:

Mix flour with sugar and salt; cut butter into flour.

Add water to make dough (add more or less water as needed); let rest for 1 hour in the refrigerator.

Take pieces of dough about the size of a golf ball, and roll to elongate dough. Then, make circles by joining both sides of the strips.

Place rosquitos on a greased or non-stick baking pan.

Bake at 350°F for about 20 minutes, or until lightly browned.

Let rosquitos cool, then dip in glaze. Set them on a dish to let glaze harden.

Glaze preparation:

Heat sugar and water in a sauce pan. When sugar dissolves, remove from heat and add food coloring.

Let syrup cool enough and dip rosquitos.

Guisadas

Serves (varies)

Dough ingredients:

2 pounds flour

1 butter or margarine stick

1 teaspoon salt (or less)

2 teaspoons sugar

Filling ingredients:

2 grated coconuts

2 teaspoons vanilla extract

2 teaspoons cinnamon

Clove to taste

Dough preparation:

Combine all dry ingredients and cut butter into flour.

Add water to make dough (add more or less water as needed), knead and shape dough into little flat cups.

Place the cups on a greased baking pan. Bake at 350°F for 30 minutes, or until golden brown.

Filling preparation:

Melt sugar with some water in a sauce pan. When sugar dissolves, add coconut, vanilla, cinnamon, and clove; cook for 30 minutes, or until mixture is thick.

Scoop filling into baked cups and put them back in the oven and bake at 350°F for 5 minutes.

Remove from oven, cool and serve.

CULTURAL NOTE: Guisadas are traditional sweets from the province of Bocas del Toro. The guisadas are also well-known in Panama City and Colon. The guisadas can be found in small Jamaican bakeries in these areas. This dessert brings back Jiwanda's childhood memories of a van that would stop on her street to sell a variety of Jamaican baked goods, including those delicious coconut guisadas.

Buñuelos de Pascua

Serves (varies)

Dough ingredients:

1 pound otoe (taro root)

1 pound camote (white sweet potato)

1 pound ñame

1 pound yuca

1 pound pumpkin

2 eggs

1 tablespoon anise

2 tablespoons soft margarine or butter

3- 4 cups flour

1 teaspoon salt

Canola oil (for frying)

Syrup ingredients:

2 cups sugar

3 cups water

2 cinnamon sticks

Zest of one large lime

Honey

Dough preparation:

Boil otoe, camote, ñame, yuca, and pumpkin until soft. Do not over cook.

When vegetables are soft; place in a large bowl and mash them.

Add the rest of ingredients to mashed vegetables and root vegetables. Make sure to check the consistency of dough when adding flour, add more flour if dough is too soft.

Make individual balls with dough. Fry in hot oil until golden brown.

Syrup preparation:

Boil water; add sugar, cinnamon stick, and lime zest. Cook and stir until the mixture turns into syrup; add some honey to taste.

Place fried buñuelos on a large plate and bathe them with syrup, before serving.

CULTURAL NOTE: *This is the original recipe of Emma González who is from San José de Las Tablas, province of Los Santos.*

Fruit Cake

(Dulce de frutas)

Serves (Makes about 5 cakes)

Ingredients:

6 cups enriched All-purpose flour

3 cups dark brown sugar

8 eggs

7 teaspoons baking powder

1 pound margarine (butter or shortening)

1 jar (28 ounces) mincemeat

Soaked fruits (see Ingredients and preparation for soaked fruits)

½ tablespoon ground cinnamon

½ tablespoon nutmeg

½ tablespoon allspice

1 tablespoon vanilla extract

1 tablespoon almond extract

1 tablespoon lemon extract

1 small can crushed pineapple in juice

1 small bottle cherries cut in halves (reserve ¼ cup of the juice from bottle)

1 cup rum

1 cup chopped walnuts

Ingredients for Soaked Fruits:

1 container (32 ounces) candied fruits (fruit cake mix)

2 boxes (15 ounces) raisins

1 cup rum

Preparing Soaked Fruits:

Put candied fruits, raisins, and rum in the food processor, this can be done in parts. Place the mixture in a glass container and soak for a week or up to a month (the longer mixture is soaked the better).

Preparation:

Preheat oven to 350°F. Grease 5 10-inch baking pans thoroughly, cut wax paper to fit bottoms and sides of pans.

Cream margarine and sugar; mix together with an electric mixer until light and fluffy; then beat in the eggs, one at a time, beating well after each addition.

Sift half of flour with baking powder and spices in to mixture.

Alternately, add flour, some soaked fruits, nuts, pineapple, cherries, and mincemeat; add juices and rum and mix well.

Do this until flour and all ingredients are used up.

Pour mixture into baking pans and bake for 1 hour, or until cakes leave the sides of the pan.

CULTURAL NOTE: *This is the original recipe of Eleanor Gale (Jiwanda's mother). The fruit cake is an important part of the Christmas celebration.*

JUICES, DRINKS, AND SHAKES

T he nation has a vast choice of fruits, juices, drinks, and shakes. Being a tropical country, Panama possesses an unusual variety of tropical fruits which are served plain as desserts and/or as *chichas or* natural juices (juice and *chichas* are used interchangeably in Panama). One can find fresh fruits, ice cream, natural tropical juices, drinks, *licuados,* and popular snacks at places called *fruterias.* Depending on the season and region, juices or *chichas* and shakes come in a variety of flavors, for instance, pineapple, passion fruit or *granadilla,* mango, banana, *grosella, jobo, mamey* (sapote/ zapote), papaya, watermelon, melon, soursop, guava, star apple or *caimito, naranjilla* (a tropical fruit whose juice has the taste of apple cider), or *chicha de marañón* (a beverage made from the fruit of a cashew tree), *chicha de nance* (a beverage made from a small tropical fruit that has culinary and beverage uses across Central and northern South America_ It has different names, and it's sometimes called "wild cherry" in Panama); *ciruelas* or *ciruelas traqueadoras* which were mistakenly called "plum" (for lack of another name) by Europeans when they arrived to the New World; *mamón* or *mamoncillo* grows in cluster similar to grapes and its skin is green in color, cracks open like an egg and it has a gelatinous yellowish pulp and a sweet-tart flavor; *manquenca* is a little known fruit found in the countryside of Panama. The *manquenca* tree blooms in July and its rare fruit is ready to be eaten in October; and of course, the always popular sugar cane, coconut, and corn juices, orange, lemon and various citrus fruit juices.

Popular drinks or juices among the Afro-Panamanian population, especially in Bocas, Colon, and parts of the province of Panama are hamony (chicheme: a beverage made of boiled corn), ginger beer, icing glass or sea moss, ice tea, and sorrel or *saril*. Equally popular are juices made of mango, ñame, ahuyama or pumpkin, michila or muogo (made of green banana), panela and ginger, beets –carrot and milk, and pixbae. Some restaurants and Panamanian families serve combination drinks made of roots and flowers like ñame and sorrel, and fruit and grain like rice and pineapple. Sorrel is usually served as a social drink for Christmas.

Herbal and hot drinks are also very popular among Panamanians, especially those hot drinks made from medicinal plants. *Marucha* or lemongrass, *yerba buena* or peppermint, melissa or lemon balm, oregano, soursop, and yanten are commonly used for making herbal teas and flavoring foods. Ginger is also a popular medicinal tea among Panamanians. The country grows its own coffee. The general believe is that the best quality Panamanian coffee comes from the mountains of Chiriqui. Most Panamanians start their days with a fresh-brewed cup of coffee. They also drink chocolate, cacao, oat, and various rice and corn-based drinks.

Chicheme

Serves 10 to 12

Ingredients:

1 pound or 2 ¾ cups cracked corn

2 cups evaporated milk

2 cups condensed milk

1 cinnamon stick

Sugar to taste

1 teaspoon vanilla (optional)

Preparation:

Put corn in water overnight.

The next day, wash and boil corn for several hours until soft. Important: Do not let dry. Keep adding enough water to cover corn.

Add cinnamon stick.

When corn is soft, remove cinnamon stick. Let cool and add sugar, vanilla, and milk. Mix well.

Serve hot or cold.

CULTURAL NOTE: Traditionally, chicheme has been made across the nation. The more conventional chicheme is seasoned with sugar and cinnamon (and/or vanilla). However, it is said that Chicheme is "the specialty drink" of La Chorrera. Today, an array of fresh tropical fruit-flavored chicheme is served in this region. Another variation of chicheme is "Hamony," the name used among Afro-Panamanians from the Bocas del Toro region (see next recipe). The above chicheme recipe is the original recipe of Nilsa and Jiwanda's relatives.

Hamony

Serves 16 to 20

Ingredients:

2 pounds cracked corn

2 cans evaporated milk

2 pounds grated coconut

4 cups sugar

1 teaspoon cloves

1 cinnamon stick

3 teaspoons vanilla

½ teaspoon nutmeg

1 cup raw rice

1-2 tablespoons cornstarch

Preparation:

Wash corn and leave in water overnight.

Next day, boil corn, cloves, and cinnamon in large pot of water.

When corn is soft add rice and continue to boil until cooked (add more water if necessary)

Add coconut milk and continue to boil for 3 minutes. For instructions on how to extract milk from coconut, see "Rice with Coconut" recipe.

Dissolve cornstarch in water.

Add sugar and cornstarch; mix well and continue to boil until it thickens.

Add evaporated milk, vanilla, and nutmeg.

Serve hot or cold.

CUTURAL NOTE: *This hamony recipe was collected by us, while traveling and interviewing Afro-Panamanians in Panama.*

TIPS: You can buy frozen grated coconut at some Latino markets or supermarkets. You can also order online.

Rice Chicheme
(Chicheme de arroz)

Serves 4 to 6

Ingredients:

1 pound chicheme rice or alboreo-style rice

3 cups water

2 cups milk

2 cloves

Cinnamon to taste

1 teaspoon vanilla

Dash salt

Sugar to taste

Preparation:

In large pot heat milk, water, sugar, salt, cloves, and vanilla. Boil for 5 minutes, stirring well.

Add rice; stir and cook on low for 20 minutes, or until rice is soft (more milk or water can be added if mix is too thick).

Serve as a hot or cold drink.

Rice and Pineapple Drink
(Chicha de arroz con piña)

Serves 6 to 8

Ingredients:

1 cup uncooked rice

1 unpeeled pineapple

6 cups milk

1 cinnamon stick

Sugar to taste

4 cups water

½ teaspoon nutmeg (optional)

Preparation:

Pour 4 cups of water in a big pot and bring it to a boil.

Peel pineapple and boil only peel. Cut pulp into chunks and reserve.

Add cinnamon stick to boiling water and boil everything until pineapple peel is soft.

Let stand for 5 to 10 minutes. Blend pineapple peel. Strain and keep only juice and discard the rest.

Cook rice in pineapple peel juice until rice is soft (add more water if necessary).

Blend rice, milk, reserved chunks of pineapple, and sugar. It's ready to drink.

Adding nutmeg and ice to blend is optional. It's a very refreshing drink!

CULTURAL NOTE: *This is the original recipe of Ofelina Lasso (Nilsa's mother). This recipe has been in the family for many years.*

NOTE: *Ever wondered what to do with the pineapple peel? Wonder no more! Take a look at this easy recipe.*

Resbaladera

Serves 6 to 8

Ingredients:

2 cups rice

1 cup barley

2 cups sugar

3 cinnamon sticks

¼ teaspoon salt

1 teaspoon vanilla

1 lime peel

10 cups water

Preparation:

Leave rice and barley soaking for about 10 to 12 hours.

Mix water, cinnamon, lime peel, and salt.

Add rice and barley and cook until tender.

Take out lime peel and cinnamon sticks; add the rest of ingredients.

Blend until smooth and creamy. Serve cold.

Sorrel Beverage

(Chicha de saril)

Serves 20

Ingredients:

4 cups dried sorrel

12 cups water

1 cinnamon stick

18 cloves

2 teaspoons orange zest

2 peeled and smashed ginger hands

Sugar to taste

Preparation:

Bring 6 cups of water to a boil in a non-reactive pot
(preferably porcelain coated or glass).

Add sorrel and the rest of ingredients.

Continue to boil on low; add the rest of water.

Boil for 10 additional minutes. Then, turn the flame off,
cover, and leave overnight.

The next day, strain and add sugar to taste (add more water if
sorrel is too strong).

 Make sure to fetch cloves and ginger and keep them in the
drink while refrigerating.

Serve with ice.

CUTURAL NOTE: *Hibiscus sabdariffa is a beautiful and edible flower with nutritional and medicinal properties. Its origin of cultivation appears to be India and Malaysia, and later carried over to Africa. It is a flower of many names: Roselle, sorrel, saril, Jamaica sorrel, Indian sorrel, sour-sour, Guinea sorrel, Queensland jelly plant, lemon bush, flor de Jamaica, Jamaica, quimbombó chino, Florida cranberry, oseille rouge, oseille de Guinée, agrio de Guinea, vinagreira, curudú azédo, quiabeiro azédo, zuring, carcadé, bisap, and others. It is commonly served as iced tea or as hot tea in Mexico, Panama, Brazil, and Guatemala. In Panama, it is a very popular cold drink during the hot summer months (December to April), especially around Christmas and New Year's Eve. In the peninsula de Azuero, Hibiscus sabdariffa grows wild in farms and home gardens. There are varieties of this recipe. The recipe above has been in Jiwanda's family for many years.*

Pineapple Peel Drink

(Chicha de cáscara de piña)

Serves 10 to 12

Ingredients:

Use the peel of two pineapples

Water

Sugar to taste

Preparation:

Put pineapple peel in a large glass jar or two smaller ones.
Fill jar up to about 3 to 4 inches from the top, cover the jar
loosely.
Leave jar on counter top for 6 days.
Strain; add more water and sugar to taste.
Serve cold.

*NOTE: Ever wondered what to do with the pineapple peel?
Wonder no more! Take a look at this easy recipe.*

Ginger Beer
(Cerveza de jengibre)

Serves 16

Ingredients:

1 pound grated ginger

1 gallon water

3 limes

1 whole clove

1 cinnamon stick

Sugar to taste

Preparation:

In a large pot, heat water on low and add grated ginger, clove, and cinnamon.

Stir and remove from stove. When warm pour in a large glass bottle and add lime juice. Leave to set for about 2 to 3 days.

Strain with cheese cloth.

Add sugar to taste and a little more lime juice for flavoring.

Serve ice cold.

Icing Glass

Serves 8 to 10

Ingredients:

1 pound Irish sea moss

2 limes

1 pack icing glass

1 cinnamon stick

1 clove

2 teaspoons ground nutmeg

1 tablespoon vanilla

1 can (12 ounces) evaporated milk

1can (14 ounces) condensed milk

Sugar to taste

Preparation:

Clean and soak sea moss with lime juice 8 to 12 hours, or overnight.

Next day, cook sea moss in boiling water until soft. Remove from heat and strain. Discard the solid materials.

Return to heat and add icing glass, cinnamon, and clove. Continue cooking until icing glass is dissolved. Remove cinnamon stick and clove.

Place in blender and add remaining ingredients.

Blend until it becomes smooth and lose. Drink may become thicker as it cools. You may want to add more evaporated milk or water to reach desired consistency.

Serve with ice.

CULTURAL NOTE: Irish moss is a type of seaweed that grows along ocean coasts. Originally, it was found near Ireland but now it's cultivated in other parts of the world. It is said to have a very high nutritional content. It is a popular ingredient in foods, drinks, and medicines. It is considered an energy booster by many. In Trinidad and Tobago, men claim it is an aphrodisiac. In Jamaica, the Jamaican sea moss drink is a traditional and popular recipe. In fact, one of the most popular versions of this drink comes from Jamaica. In Panama, "icing glass" is a popular variation of the Caribbean sea moss drinks. It is usually prepared and served in the Afro-Panamanian communities of Bocas del Toro, Colon, and Panama City.

Nance Drink
(Chicha de nance)

Serves 4 to 6

Ingredients:

4 cups *nance*

4 cups water

½ cup sugar

2 teaspoons pure vanilla extract (optional)

Preparation:

Extract pulp by squeezing nances. Discard nance seeds.

Strain; add water, sugar, and vanilla. Add more sugar, if desired. Mix well.

Refrigerate and serve cold.

CULTURAL NOTE: During the summer months, Panamanians will most likely offer you a glass of this refreshing drink. Duros de nance or popsicles are made of nance juice. Many Panamanians sell nance popsicles in cups from their homes. Both, nance drink and nance popsicles are undeniably very popular among Panamanians, especially school kids.

Guava Drink
(Chicha de guayaba)

Serves 6 to 8

Ingredients:

1 pound ripe guavas

1 cup sugar

4 cups cold water

Preparation:

Cut guavas in quarters and remove seeds.

Mash pulp and strain; add sugar and water.

Serve cold and garnish with lemon slices.

Banana Shake

Serves 4

Ingredients:

2 ripe bananas

2 cups milk

½ cup sugar

1 cup ice

Cinnamon powder to taste

Preparation:

Cut banana in rounds.

Place banana rounds, sugar, and milk in blender; add ice slowly and blend together.

Serve cold and sprinkle cinnamon power on top.

Papaya Shake

Serves 6 to 8

Ingredients:

2 cups ripe papaya pulp

½ cup sugar

1 cup water

3 cups milk

2 cups ice

Preparation:

Put pulp, sugar, and water in blender; add milk and ice slowly and blend together.

Serve cold and enjoy this creamy drink.

TIPS: To make papaya drink, mix 2 cups papaya pulp, 1 cup sugar. Add 4 cups of water slowly and strain. Serve cold.

Mango Drink
(Chicha de mango)

Serves 4 to 6

Ingredients:

1½ cups ripe mango pulp

1½ cups water

Sugar to taste

Ice

Preparation:

Put pulp, sugar in blender; add water and ice slowly and blend together.

Serve cold and enjoy this creamy drink.

Pineapple Drink
(Chicha de piña)

Serves 6 to 8

Ingredients:

2 cups water

4 cups fresh pineapple juice

1 cup sugar

Orange slices (for decorating)

Preparation:

Boil water and sugar for about 5 to 10 minutes and let cool; add pineapple juice.

Serve cold and garnish with orange slices.

Limeade
(Limonada)

Serves 6 to 8

Ingredients:

6 large limes

1 cup sugar

6 cups water

Preparation:

Squeeze limes. Mix sugar and water; add lime juice and serve cold.

Sweet Lime Drink
(Chicha de lima)

Serves 6 to 8

Ingredients:

6 large sweet limes

1 cup cane syrup

3 cups water

Preparation:

Squeeze sweet limes. Mix cane syrup and water; add sweet lime juice and serve cold.

Passion Fruit Beverage
(Chicha de maracuyá)

Serves 6 to 8

Ingredients:

6 ripe passion fruits

Sugar to taste

Water (as needed)

Preparation:

Cut passion fruit in half and scoop out pulp, place in blender.

Add 3 times the amount of water and blend for about 2 minutes.

Strain and discard seeds.

Add small amounts of water to soften the flavor, but do it cautiously to make sure the drink is not too strong or too weak for your taste.

Add sugar to taste and serve with ice.

Tamarind Drink
(Chicha de tamarindo)

Serves 8 to 10

Ingredients:

½ pound tamarind pods

1 ½ cups sugar

6 cups water

Preparation:

Remove seeds from pod. Mash pulp and discard seeds.

Add sugar to pulp and mix well; add water and strain.

Serve cool.

Soursop Drink
(Chicha de guanábana)

Serves 6 to 8

Ingredients:

4 cups water

1 ½ cups sugar

3 cups soursop pulp

3 teaspoons lemon juice

Preparation:

Mash soursop pulp and mix with sugar; add water and strain.

Add lemon juice and serve cold.

NOTE: To create a creamy soursop drink, add milk to taste and omit lemon juice.

Lime and Panela Drink
(Chicha de limón y raspadura)

Serves 6 to 8

Ingredients:

1 pound raspadura round (panela)

8 medium limes

6 cups water

Preparation:

Place panela in large pitcher with water to dissolve. It might take a couple hours.

Squeeze limes; add juice to pitcher and mix well.

Serve cold.

CULTURAL NOTE: Panela is a solid piece of raw sugar obtained from the boiling and evaporation of sugar cane juice. The sugar cane juice (or guarapo) is boiled again and again in large copper pots until a thick syrup is produced. It is then poured into molds to form solid pieces of raw sugar. This unrefined whole cane sugar is used as a natural sweetener for desserts and beverages. It is said to be healthier than refined sugar because it has less calories. Panela is typical of

Mexico, Central and South America. Colombia is known as the main producer of panela. This product has different names, depending on where you are. Panela (Colombia), Chancaca (Peru), piloncillo (Mexico), rapadura (Brazil), raspadura (Panama), and many more. This product can be found in most Latino stores or markets, and some regular supermarkets that carry ethnic foods in the U.S.A. or it can be ordered online. Some of the most popular brands found in the U.S.A are Goya, Nativo, and El Ideal Panela.

Guarapo Drink
(Guarapo)

Serves 6

Ingredients:

6-8 cups freshly squeezed sugar cane juice

Preparation:

Panamanians squeeze the juice out of sugar cane using a machine known as *trapiche* (sugar mill) powered, either by a horse or a person.

CULTURAL NOTE: This process usually involves a sugar mill or a large commercial juicer. However, people can use a regular juicer and extract sugar cane juice in their own kitchens by washing sugar cane to remove the dirt, cutting off its outer husk, and cutting it into thin strips, lengthwise. Of course, the traditional way is much preferred by Panamanians. In Panama, this drink is very popular during the hot summer months because it's extremely refreshing. Many Panamanians claim that sugar cane has healing properties. For example, they believe sugar cane can treat conditions like urinary tract infections, constipation, low blood pressure, coughing/bronchitis and heart conditions.

Some of these claims have been scientifically proven. Farmers usually serve fermented guarapo to workers and guests at gatherings during harvesting season, at local agricultural fairs or parties. In the U.S.A., people can buy guarapo at Latin American markets or at regular supermarkets that carry ingredients for Hispanic dishes.

Cashew Apple Drink

(Chicha de marañón)

Serves 4 to 6

Ingredients:

10 Marañones (cashew apples)

Sugar to taste

Water to taste

Preparation:

Cut fruit up, and past it through a juicer. If you don't have a juicer put fruit in a blender with water.

Strain pulp to separate from juice. Discard pulp.

Add water and sugar to taste. Serve cold

Mamey Sapote Drink
(Chicha de mamey)

Serves 6 to 8

Ingredients:

2 cups ripe mamey pulp

2 cups milk

2 cups ice

Sugar to taste

Water (if necessary)

Preparation:

Put pulp and sugar in blender; add milk and ice slowly and blend together.

Add water according to personal taste.

Serve cold.

Naranjilla Beverage
(Bebida de naranjilla)

Serves 4

Ingredients:

3 ripe naranjillas

Sugar to taste

Water to taste

Preparation:

Use an orange juicer to squeeze juice out of naranjilla; add water and sugar.

OR peel naranjilla and put in a blender with two cups of water and half cup sugar.

Strain and serve with ice.

Chicha de Jobo

Serves 4

Ingredients:

Jobo

Sugar to taste

Water to taste

Preparation:

Wash fruit and separate pulp from seeds with hands.

Pass through a strainer and add water and sugar to taste.

Serve cold or over ice.

Pixbae Drink

Serves 6 to 8

Ingredients:

12 pixbaes

4 cups water

Milk to taste

Sugar to taste

Vanilla to taste

Cinnamon powder to taste

Preparation:

In a medium pot ½ full of water, cook pixbaes until soft; Peel pixbaes.

In a blender add pixbae pulp, 4 cups of water and all ingredients; blend until mixture is liquefied. Add more water and sugar, if desired.

Refrigerate before serving.

Raspadura and Ginger Drink
(Chicha de raspadura y jengibre)

Serves 6

Ingredients:

2 pounds raspadura rounds (panela)

½ pound ginger root

8 cups water

Preparation:

Boil 8 cups of water over medium-low heat; add ginger and cook for about 15 to 20 minutes, or until boiling ginger is of the concentration you desire. Basically, the longer you boil ginger, the stronger the extract becomes.

Brake panela into more manageable pieces and dissolve it in ginger extract and mix well.

Refrigerate before serving.

Chicha Mamita

Serves 4

Ingredients:

6-8 green bananas

Milk to taste

Sugar to taste

Preparation:

Boil green bananas. Remove and blend for a few minutes; add milk and sugar to taste.

Raspado or Raspao'

Serves (varies)

Ingredients:

1 small ice block (or 2 ice trays regular ice cubes)

Fruit -flavored syrup (your favorite)

1 can (12 ounces) condensed milk

2 cups cane syrup

12 cone-shaped paper cups

Preparation:

Shave ice block with an ice shaver machine (or snow cone machine) or crush regular ice cubes in an ice-crushing blender.

Place shaved or crushed ice in individual cone-shaped paper cups.

Pour your favorite fruit-flavored syrup over it (you can use a syrup dispenser bottle).

Drizzle condensed milk and cane syrup over the top and enjoy!

CULTURAL NOTE: *A Raspado is a snow cone. It is without a doubt one of Panama's favorite refreshing snacks, especially during the hot summer months. Raspados are normally sold by street vendors from their mobile carts or stands. There is a good variety of fruit-flavored syrups. Panamanians love drizzling condensed milk and/or cane syrup over the top of their snow cones.*

Lemongrass, Peppermint, Oregano, or Soursop Leaf Tea

(Té de hierba de limón, yerba buena, orégano u hoja de guanábana)

Serves 1

Ingredients:

3 leaves (of chosen herb)

1 cup water

2 teaspoons sugar (optional)

Preparation:

Wash leaves thoroughly. Bring water to a boil and add leaves. Add sugar if desired.

Drink hot or warm.

Ginger Tea
(Té de jengibre)

Serves 4 to 6

Ingredients:

4 2-inch pieces ginger root

4-5 cups water

Preparation:

Wash root thoroughly. Cut into long thin strips.

In a medium pot, boil water and add ginger strips. Cover and cook for about 20 to 25 minutes, or until ginger has dissolved its essence.

Strain and serve warm.

Cashew Coffee
(Café de pepita de marañón)

Serves 8

Ingredients:

½ pound roasted cashews

Evaporated milk to taste

Sugar to taste

Preparation:

Grind cashews in a grinder or a food processor to make a powder.

To make coffee: boil one cup of water and add 2 tablespoons of cashew powder.

Add milk and sugar; continue to boil for a few minutes on low.

Strain and serve.

ALCOHOLIC DRINKS

Aselection of quality domestic alcoholic beverages is also offered across Panama. The best known rums are *Ron Abuelo (añejo, 7 years, 12 years), Carta Vieja (añejo, clear and extra clear),* and *Cortez (añejo, white, gold, and spiced).* All these rums are made from nationally-grown sugar cane. *Carta Vieja* is produced in the Chiriqui Province. *Abuelo* and *Cortez* are produced by one of the major distilleries in the nation. Panamanians also consume gin and the most popular is *Gin Caballito* made from sugar cane juice, a mixture of sweeteners, natural citrics and juniper flavors. *Balboa, Panama, Soberana, and Atlas* are the most well-known Panamanian beers. Imported beers are also very popular. Surprisingly, Panama produces natural organic wine but not from grapes. Its wine is made from a variety of fruits, such as raspberry, passion fruit, strawberry, and others found in the highlands of Chiriqui province. In fact, Panamanian wine has been recognized internationally. For instance, the raspberry dessert wine produced by Panamanian wine makers *Vinos Tropicales* (Tropical Wines) won the Golden Medal at an International Wine Expo in 2003.

Alcoholic beverages are always on hand, especially during holidays and local celebrations. *Seco Herrerano* is the Panamanian national liquor. *Seco* is a dry clear liquid made from fermented sugar cane. It can be used as a replacement for rum or vodka and it's commonly served with milk and ice. *Seco* is heavily produced in the province of Herrera.

Other well-liked drinks among country people are palm tree wine, fermented *guarapo* (sugar cane juice), rum punch, *chirrisco, mistela, chicha de corozo, chicha bruja* and *chicha fuerte of maize* or *chicha de junta. Chicha* of maize is the refreshment of choice during and after community work parties, as well as community dances like *tamboritos. Chicha bruja* is made of seaweed and cane syrup and it appears to have medicinal values. Rum punch is usually served at Christmas and New Year's dinners.   Both *chirrisco* and *mistela* are prepared with fermented sugar cane juice and are well-liked in the province of Veraguas. *Chicha corozo* and palm tree wine are also very popular in Veraguas.   In most provinces, it's customary to serve egg nog and *piña colada* during the holidays, particularly in the provinces of Panama, Colon and Bocas del Toro.

Fermented Corn Drink

(Chicha de maíz fermentado)

Serves (varies)

Ingredients:

1 pound mature corn kernels

½ cup sugar cane juice or 1 pound panela block

5-6 gallons water

6 cups of sugar (or to taste)

5 orange leaves (optional)

Preparation:

Need plenty of water for cleaning, soaking, cooking, and thinning.

Clean corn well; place in water to soak overnight.

Next day, drain water and wash corn in fresh water; grind corn into a paste (use a corn grinder or a food processor).

Clean paste, removing any pieces of husk, if any; place paste in a large pot and add 1 gallon of water. Bring to a boil.

Stir occasionally to prevent it from sticking to the bottom of the pot. When corn is cooked, let cool.

Mix sugar cane juice with ½ gallon of water (or dissolve panela block in 1 gallon of water) and stir liquid into corn paste.

Add five orange leaves.

Pour into large plastic container and cover with lid.

Serve next day or allow to ferment at room temperature 3 to 4 days.

TIPS: *If you want it a bit spicy or fermented, do not uncover for 3-4 days. Mix the sweetened corn with 1 gallon of water. Stir in sugar and serve.*

NOTE: *A variation to the original recipe: add vanilla and refrigerate.*

Sprouted Corn Drink

(Chicha de maíz nacido)

Serves (varies)

Ingredients:

1 pound mature corn kernels

2 panela blocks or 2½ cups raw sugar

1 lemon

Preparation:

Soak corn in water overnight.

Next day, wash corn and sprinkle with lemon juice; leave to germinate 3 to 4 days, rinsing it each day.

Grind or process germinated corn in a food processor; cook for 1 hour and let cool. Allow to ferment at room temperature 2 days.

Cook again for 1 hour and add raw sugar or panela (if panela is used, break block into smaller pieces before adding).

Let cool, strain and serve.

Chicha Loja

Serves 20 to 25

Ingredients:

2 pounds cracked corn

8 bitter orange leaves

1 solid block panela

1 teaspoon allspice

2 cinnamon sticks

6 cloves

1 small ginger root

4 gallons water

Preparation:

In a large cast iron pot, toast corn over high heat, stirring constantly to prevent burning.

Add water and bring to a boil; lower heat and simmer 3 to 4 hours, or until corn is soft.

Let cool, strain corn, and reserve liquid.

Grind or process corn in a corn grinder or a food processor and mix with reserved liquid.

Add remaining ingredients and cook for 3 additional hours.

Let cool and strain once again.

Keep only liquid and store in 5-gallon plastic buckets; allow to ferment at room temperature 3 to 4 days.

Egg Nog (Cooked)
(Ron ponche)

Serves 10 to 12

Ingredients:

1 ½ cups sugar

1 can (12 ounces) evaporated milk

1 can (12 ounces) condensed milk

3 cups water

1 ½ tablespoons cornstarch

1 teaspoon pure vanilla extract

2 cups rum

12 beaten egg yolks

Preparation:

In a large pot, mix all ingredients, except egg yolks and rum; cook, stirring consistently until it begins to boil.

Remove mixture from heat; add 1 serving spoon of mixture to beaten egg yolks. Then, slowly add beaten egg yolks to cooked mixture, stirring continuously so that eggs will not cook. Stir until mixed thoroughly.

Let cool and add rum. Stir again and store in refrigerator.

Serve in small glasses.

Egg Nog (Uncooked)
(Ron ponche)

Serves 10 to 12

Ingredients:

8 whole eggs

3 cans (12 ounces) evaporated milk

2 cans (12 ounces) condensed milk

2 cups rum

1 teaspoon ground cinnamon or ground cloves

Preparation:

Beat eggs well with an electric mixer on medium speed.

Add evaporated and condensed milk, then rum. Mix well.

Store in glass bottles and refrigerate.

Serve in small glasses and sprinkle ground cinnamon or cloves on top.

Tropical Sangria
(Sangría tropical)

Serves 8 to 10

Ingredients:

1 bottle dry red wine

¼ cup raw sugar

4 cinnamon sticks

1 cup fresh orange juice

1 seeded and thinly sliced large orange

1 seeded and thinly sliced lime

1 peeled and cubed mango

2 cups peeled pineapple chunks

1 thinly sliced kiwi

2 cups club soda

Preparation:

Mix wine, sugar, and cinnamon sticks; stir with a wooden spoon until sugar dissolves.

Add all fruits. Let stand for 30 minutes.

Add club soda, mix, and serve. Add more sugar, if desired.

Serve with crushed ice in wine glasses.

The Panamanian Soother

Serves 8 to 10

Ingredients:

1 ½ cups *Ron Abuelo Añejo*

½ cup fresh orange juice

1 ounce agave nectar

1 pack fresh blueberries

12 sage leaves

2 bottles ginger beer

Preparation:

In a large pitcher, muddle berries and sage together.

Add remaining ingredients and ice; stir very well and serve.

Seco Herrerano with Milk

(Seco con leche)

Serves 4

Ingredients:

1 cup Seco (sugar cane liquor)

½ cup milk

Preparation:

In a small pitcher, add all ingredients and stir very well. Serve over ice.

Chichita

Serves 10

Ingredients:

1 liter pineapple juice

2 cups grapefruit juice

1 ¼ cups Seco (sugar cane liquor)

¼ cup grenadine

½ cup sugar

Orange slices (for decoration)

Preparation:

In a large pitcher, add all ingredients and stir very well. Serve in glasses with ice and orange slices.

Basil Martini

(Martini de albahaca)

Serves 1

Ingredients:

1 ounce *Seco Herrerano* (sugar cane liquor)

Splash lime juice

1 ounce Triple Sec

3 basil leaves

1 green apple slice

Lime peel (for decoration)

Preparation:

Mix all ingredients, except lime peel.

Serve over crushed ice and garnish with lime peel.

Mojito of the House

(Mojito de la casa)

Serves 1

Ingredients:

1.5 ounces dark rum

Raw sugar to taste

12 mint leaves

Lemongrass to taste

Splash club soda

1 sliced small lime (3 pieces)

Preparation:

Macerate lime, lemongrass, sugar, and mint together in a glass.

Add ice, and remaining ingredients; mix and serve.

Seco Sour

Serves 1

Ingredients:

3 onces Seco (sugar cane liquor)

2 ½ ounces sweet and sour mix

Lime wedge (for decoration)

Preparation:

In a 'shaker' pour Seco and sweet and sour.

Add ice and shake mix to cool.

Pour in a glass with ice, and garnish with lime wedge, carefully sliding wedge onto the rim of the glass.

Dirty Mojito

Serves 1

Ingredients:

2 ounces *Ron Abuelo*

8 mint leaves

3 lime wedges

2 ¼ teaspoons sugar

Splash lemon-lime soda (Sprite)

Preparation:

In a shaker add lime wedges, mint leaves, and sugar.

With a mortar, macerate all three ingredients until a little lime juice comes out.

Add *Ron Abuelo*, ice to taste, and lemon-lime soda; shake well and serve.

Panama Lord

Serves 1

Ingredients:

2 ounces *Ron Abuelo Añejo*

1 ounce lime juice

Ice Tea (sweet or unsweetened)

Lime wedge (garnish)

Preparation:

In a tall glass with ice, pour rum and lime juice; shake well.

Top off with ice tea and garnish with lime wedge.

REPUBLIC OF PANAMA

QUICK FACTS AND TIPS

FOR TRAVELERS

https://www.cia.gov/library/publications/
the-world-factbook/geos/pm.html

Flag Day in Panama is celebrated on November 4

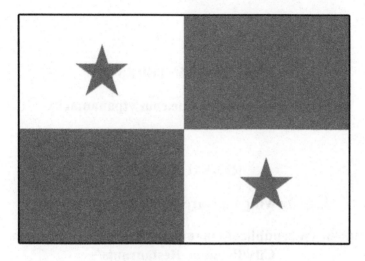

Designed by Manuel E. Amador
The first flag was made by Mrs. María Ossa de Amador

The Panama flag is a rectangle that is divided into four squares. The top left hand quarter is white with a blue star in the center, the top right quarter is solid red, the bottom left hand quarter is solid blue, and the bottom right hand quarter is white with a five-pointed red star in the center. The red and blue colors represent the political parties: Liberal (red) and Conservative (blue). The combination of the colors symbolizes peace, harmony, and union of the parties. The two stars combined stood for the new republic but they also have a special meaning of their own. The blue star simbolyzes purity and honesty and the red star stands for Panama's authority and law.

PLACES OF INTERESTS

http://www.vtoursonline.com/vtpanamacity/

RESTAURANTS

http://www.panamarestaurantsreview.com/

http://www.republicofpanama.net/Restaurants/Panama_City/Panama_Restaurants/

HOTELS AND RESORTS

http://www.panamaresorts.com/hotels/index.htm

SPECIAL HOLIDAYS AND CELEBRATIONS

Janurary - February

New Year's (Jan. 1)

Canajagua Folkloric Festival, Los Santos Province

Martyr's Day (U.S./Panama Conflict over Panama Canal, (Jan. 9)

Christ of Esquipulas of Anton Festival, Anton, Cocle (Jan. 15)

International Fair of the Flowers and Coffee, Boquete, Chiriqui Province

Tanara Fair, Chepo, Panama Province

Fair of St. Sebastian, Ocu, Herrera Province

International Fair of La Chorrera, Panama Province

Homemade Desserts Fair of San Francisco de La Montaña, Vergaguas Province

Fair of the Orange, Churuquita Grande, Penonome, Cocle Province

Fair of La Candelaria, Bugaba, Chiriqui Province

Fair of Santa Fe, Veraguas Province

Fair of Sona, Veraguas Province

Jesus of Nazareth, Atalaya, Veraguas Province

Fair of Turism at Albrook Mall, Panama Province

Carnival Celebrations (Moving Date Tuesday Carnival, the day before Ash Wednesday). Carnival takes place 40 days before the Christian Holy Week. For more information check online (Feb.-Mar.)

The Great West Indian Fair, Panama City, Panama Province (it takes place during Carnival).

Ash Wednesday to Palm Sunday – Christ of Atalaya or "El Nazareth" processions, Atalaya, Veraguas

March-April

"Semana Santa" Holy Week in Panama (Moving Date Good Friday). For more information go online.

Diablos y Congos Festival, Chepigana, Darien Province

Fair of Santa Fe, Darien Province

Fair of Chitra (Calobre), Veraguas Province

The San Jose International Fair, David, Chiriqui Province

The San Jose Fair of Tole, Chiriqui Province

The ExpoCosta Fair of Nuevo Tonosi, Colon Province

El Colmon Fair, Macaracas, Los Santos Province

The National Sugar Cane Festival, Pese, Herrera Province (Feb. or Mar.)

Festival Bulla y Bullerengue, Darien Province

Diablos y Congos of Portobelo, Colon Province

National Fair of Colon, Colon Province

Valle de Tonosi Fair, Los Santos Province

Fair of the Orquids, Boquete, Chiriqui Province

Villa del Rosario Fair, Capira, Panama Province

The International Azuero Fair, Los Santos Province

The Guacho en Totuma, Atalaya,Veraguas Province.
(This is an annual festival that takes place in April or May).

May-June

Labor Day (May 1)

Feast Day of Corpus Christi, Taboga Island. (This is a Christian feast in honor of Holy Eucharist. Each year it falls on a different day - May or June).

San Antonio de Padua, Puerto Armuelles, Chiriqui Province.

Corpus Christi Festival, Los Santos Province (it is held 60 days after Easter).

Father's Day (Second Sunday in June).

July-August

La Pollera Festival of Las Tablas, Los Santos Province

Festival of Mono en Bijao de Bugaba, Chiriqui Province

Santa Librada Celebrations, Los Santos Province

National Handicraft Fair

Manito de Ocu Festival, Herrera Province

Founder's Day of Old Panama City (Aug. 15)

September-October

Fair of the Holy Spirit Flower, Las Minas, Herrera Province

Founder's Day of the Town of Sona, Veraguas Province (Sept. 12)

Sea Fair, Bocas del Toro Province

La Mejorana Festival (folkloric festival), **Los Santos Province**

International Day of Turism (celebrated across the nation – Sept. 27)

Fair of Changuinola, Bocas del Toro Province

Fair of Camaron Arriba Santa Rosa, Bugaba, Chiriqui Province

Fair of Tiger Island, San Blas, Indigenous Territory or Comarca

Torito Guapo Festival, Anton, Cocle Province

Rambala Fair, Bocas del Toro Province

Founder's Day of Chitre District, Herrera Province (Oct. 19)

Black Christ of Portobelo Festival, Portobelo, Colon Province (Oct. 21)

Rio Sereno Coffee Festival, Chiriqui Province

Typical/Folkloric Parade (Oct. 24), **Founder's Day of Chitre City, Herrera Province** (Oct. 19)

November-December

Independence Day (from Colombia, 1903 – Nov. 3)

Flag Day (Nov. 4)

Civic Parade, David, Chiriqui Province (Nov. 10)

First Call for Independence from Spain in Villa de Los Santos (Nov. 10)

Mi Ranchito de Rio de Jesus Festival, Veraguas Province

Emancipation (from Spain, 1821 – Nov. 28)

Fair of St. Andrews, Bugaba, Chiriqui Province

Mother's Day (Dec. 8)

Fair of the Highlands in Volcan, Chiriqui Province

Christmas (Dec. 25)

New Year's Eve (Dec. 31)

Note: These are some of the most important celebrations/ holidays, religious festivals, and regional and international fairs. In Panama, every town and region has its own annual religious celebration dedicated to a patron saint. These special days provide a way to experience Panamanian folklore, culture, history, tradition, and beliefs.

TYPICAL MENUS
Breakfast

Corn Tortilla or Changa

White Cheese

Coffee and/or Milk

Orange Juice

Hojaldres or local bread

Beef with Onion

Coffee and/or Milk

Papaya

Corn Bollos

Eggs

White Cheese

Coffee and/or Milk

Fruit in season

Corn bollos or local bread

Chicharrón (pork rinds) or Roast Pork

Coffee and/or Milk

Grapefruit Juice

Fruit in season

Egg bread

White cheese

Cuchifrito (organ meats)

Coffee and/or milk

Orange juice

Micha Bread

Liver and Onions

Pineapple Slices

Coffee and/or Milk

Orange or Pineapple Juice

Tortilla or Changa with White Cheese

Or

Tortilla with National Chorizos

Coffee, Milk or any Tropical Fruit Juice

Bollos and National Chorizos

Or

Chicharrones (pork rinds) with Chunks of Boiled Yuca

Note: The preferred cheese for a typical breakfast is fresh white pressed cheese. In some households in rural areas, people serve rice for breakfast (usually left over rice from the day before).

TYPICAL MENUS

(Special Occasions)

Rice with Chicken

Avocado Salad

Plantain in Temptation or Tajadas

Cocada

Coffee

Soursop Drink

Guacho

Tasajo and Onions

Yuca al Mojo with butter

Suspiros

Coffee

Rice and Pineapple Shake

Sancocho

Fried Yuca

Beef on the Stick

Coffee

Chicheme

Guacho de Marisco

Fried Yuca or Twice-Fried Plantains

Avocado and Shrimp Salad

Meringues

Coffee

Tamarind Drink

Tamales

BBQ Beef or Beef on the Stick

BBQ Chicken

Potato Salad

Baked Plantain or Tajadas, Rice Pudding

Coffee, Tamarind Drink or Sorrel Beverage

Seafood Combination Soup

Rice with Clams

Stuffed Fish

Yuca Salad

Tropical Juices, Coffee

Red Bean Pie

Resbaladera

White Rice

Beef and Tomato

Tajadas

Sour Orange Candy

Coffee

Papaya Drink

Rice with Coconut or Rice with Shrimp

Or/Pig tails

Pork Ribs

Carrots and Beets Salad

Ripe Plantain Pie

Coffee

Nance Drink

MENU

(Typical Wedding)

Rice with Chicken

Roast Pork

Tamales

Bollos Changos, Mature Corn Bollos and

Bollos de Chicharrón

Twice-Fried Plantains

Fried Yuca

Tortilla and Coffee

Beef on the Stick

Tamarind Drink

Corn Drink or Fermented Corn Drink

Cocada

Suspiros

Meringues

Sopa Borracha

Sopa de Gloria

BIBLIOGRAPHY

Acuña, Oliva María and Dolores de Scotland. *Recipes from the West Indian Cuisine*. Panama, Republic of Panama, 1999.

ADMIN. "Passion Fruit Names." *Antioxidant-fruits.com*, 20 Dec. 2009. Web. 21 Jun. 2012.

Administrator, "Al estilo panameño." Bar Selecto. *Selecta Magazine Online*. Magazine and Design Group S.A. n.d. Web. 2011.

"Ají chombo." *Thechileman.org*. The Chili Pepper Company, 1996. Web. 30 Apr. 2012.

Alfaro, Ana. "El pan de Dios." *Prensa.com*. La Prensa, 19 Sept. 2007. Web. 2 Mar. 2011.

Anthony Bourdain: No Reservations. Panama. Narr. Anthony Bourdain. Travel Channel. 12 Apr. 2010.

Araúz, Hernán, Personal Interview. 23 October 2010.

"A Short Guide to Panamanian Typical Food." *Focuspublicationsint.com*. Panamanian Food, Focus Panama, n.d. Web. 18 May 2010.

Aspectos técnicos sobre cuarenta y cinco cultivos agrícolas de Costa Rica. Dirección General de Investigación y Extensión Agrícola. Ministerio de Agricultura y Ganadería: San José, 1991.

"A traditional Taste of Panama: Tule Masi." *Amble.com*. Amble Resorts, 8 Jan. 2012. Web. 23 Jan. 2012.

Bell, Eleanor Y. "Las razas y sus mezclas (1909)." *Panamá en sus usos y costumbres.* Ed. Stanley Heckadon Moreno. Tomo 14, Panama: Editorial Universitaria, 1994. 19-22.

"Best Countries for Business: #60 Panama." *Forbes.com.* Forbes, n.d. Web. 30 Mar. 2012.

Billingslea, Dora de. *100 Recetas Típicas Panameñas.* Editorial Géminis, 2002.

British and Committee (Ladies) Panama and Colon. 2nd ed. Panama: The Panama American Publishing Co., 1941.

Burr, Fearing. (2007). *The Field and Garden Vegetables of America.* Available from http://www.gutenberg.org/ebooks/21682.

Camarena, Luis Alberto. "La Bollada." *Folklore. PanamaTipico.com,* n.d. Web. 1 Mar. 2012.

Center for New Crops & Plant Products. *Hort.purdue.edu.* Purde University, 10 Dec. 2011. Web. 1995.

Chang Vargas, Giselle. Introduction. *Nuestras Comidas* 3-17. San José: Coordinación Educativa y Cultural Centroamericana (CECC), Serie Culturas Populares Centroamericanas, No. 4, 2001.

Comité Agrícola. XLVI Feria Internacional de San Jose de David. *Recetario Panameño.* 2001.

Corella R., José A. *Panamá: Algo de lo Nuestro.* Chiriquí, Rep. de Panamá, 2001.

Corrigan, Damian. "Introduction to Paella: The History of Paella and Paella Today." *About.com Guide Spain Travel.* About.com, n.d. Web. 6 Mar. 2012.

De Castro, Woodrow. "Los judíos en Panamá (1992)." *Panamá en sus usos y costumbres.* Ed. Stanley Heckadon Moreno. Tomo 14, Panama: Editorial Universitaria, 1994. 95-107.

"Deep History of Coconut Decoded: Origins of Cultivation, Ancient Trade Routes, and Colonization of the Americas." *ScienceDaily.com,* 24 Jun. 2011. Web. 12 Jun. 2012.

De La Cruz, Maribel. Personal Interview. 17 November 2010.

De La Cruz, Serafín. Personal Interview. 17 November 2010.

De León, Melissa. "Delicious Lost Desserts from Panama: Bienmesabe Chiricano." *Cooking diva.net,* 24 May 2011. Web. 4 Dec. 2011.

Demetri, Justin. "Italian Pasta Through the Ages." *Life in Italy.com,* n.d. Web. 27 Mar. 2012.

Didimay. "Comidas Panameñas: recetas de cocina y comida de Panamá, las recetas secretas, un buen legado." *Blogspot. com.* Booster Blog, 6 Jun. 2011. Web. 9 Apr. 2012.

"Differences between Cane Syrup & Molasses." *eHow.* Demand Media Inc., 1999-2012. Web. 5 May 2012.

El Presidente de la República y El Ministro de Economía y Comercio. *Norma Oficial de Nomenclatura de Frutos y Productos Hortícolas.* La Gaceta No. 202, 25 de octubre 1990. San José.

"Ensalada de Coditos." *Recetas y Comidas.com.* Recetas y Comidas Cocina Panamá, n.d. Web. 10 Oct. 2011.

"Ensalada de Zapallo." *Recetas y Comidas.com.* Recetas y Comidas Cocina Panamá, n.d. Web. 10 Oct. 2011.

"Escoviched Red Snapper." *The Panama News: English-language Online Newspaper.* The Panama News Mag., Vol. 10, No. 3, 8 Feb. 2004. Web 2 Mar. 2011.

"Fufu or Fish Soup with Coconut Milk." *arecetas.com.* Arecetas, n.d. Web. 28 Feb. 2012.

Gale, Catherine. Letters (with recipes) to the authors. 12 Apr. 2012.

Gale, Eleanor. Personal Interviews. 18 October 2011 and 20 March 2012.

Gibbs Ostmann, Barbara, and Jane L. Baker, ed. *The Recipe Writer's Handbook.* John Wiley & Sons, INC. New York, 2001.

Gobierno Nacional, República de Panamá. *IMA.* Instituto de Mercadeo Agropecuario. n.d. Web 10 May 2012.

González, Emma. Letters (with recipes) to the authors. 10 April, 2012.

Grinard, Migdalia. " Bon , la tradición del pan para Semana Santa en Colón." *prensa.com.* Prensa.com, 7 April 2007. Web. 20 Mar. 2012.

Gutiérrez, Arquímedez. Personal Interview. 15 April 2011.

Gutiérrez, Aurora. Personal Interview. 14 November 2010.

Gutiérrez, Florencio. Personal Interview. 14 November 2010.

Gutiérrez, Xenia. Personal Interview. 23 November 2010 and 18 October 2011.

Hemphill, Ian. *The Spice and Herb Bible: A Cook's Guide.* 2000. Toronto: Robert Rose Inc.2002.Print.

"History of Chinese Noodles." *Cheftalk.com*, n.d. Web. 27 Mar. 2012.

"How to Make Panamanian Chicken Fried Rice." *eHow*. Demand Media, Inc., n.d. Web. 1 Jun. 2011.

"How to Make Panamanian Potato Salad." *eHow*. Demand Media, Inc., n.d. Web. 1 Jun. 2011.

"How to Make White Rice Like They Do in Panama." *eHow*. Demand Media, Inc., n.d. Web. 1 Jun. 2011.

Hubbard, Kristin. "Panama Food and Drinks." *About.com Guide Central America Travel*. About.com, n.d. Web. 5 Feb. 2012.

Jaén Espinosa, Marino. "Bun: An Afro-Caribbean Bread in Panama." *Folklore.PanamaTipico.com*, 12 Apr. 2009. Web. 20 Apr. 2012.

---. "What is a *Matanza*?" *Folklore.PanamaTipico.com*, 2 Mar. 2005. Web. 20 Apr. 2012.

Kiple, Kenneth F., and Kriemhild Coneè Ornelas, ed. *The Cambridge World History of Food.* Cambridge University Press, 2000.

Kitchen Butterfly. "Kitchen Butterfly, World Flavor Bite by Bite": Pan Micha from Panama, Une Miche from France." *kitchenbutterfly.com*. Kitchen Butterfly, Ozoz Sokoh, 11 Jan. 2011. Web 15 Jun. 2011.

La *cocina de descubriendo a Panamá*. FE TV, Abriendo Horizontes, n.d. N. pag.

Lasso, Ofelina. Personal Interview. 10 and 20 December 2011

Marriot de Brid, Melva. *Cocina típica de Bocas del Toro:*

Recetas Panameña con sabor Afro-Antillano. Cultural Portobelo, 2008.

Martin. "Cooking and Recipes: Guisadas, Johnnycake." *Martin Central.* Geocities, n.d. Web. 9 Apr. 2012.

Mateljan, George. The World's Healthiest Foods. The George Mateljan Foundation for the World's Healthiest Foods 2001-2012. Web. 5 May 2012.

Melissa's. "Melissa's The Fresh Ideas in Produce." *Melissas. com*, 31 Jul. 2008. Web. 14 Feb. 2012.

Mon P., Ramón A. "La migración china en Panamá." *Panamá en sus usos y costumbres.* Ed. Stanley Heckadon Moreno. Tomo 14, Panama: Editorial Universitaria, 1994. 53-91.

Moon, Freda. "36 hours in Panama City, Panama." *The New York Times* 21 Apr. 2011.

Oviero, Ramón. "Panamá: Alimentos de origen precolombino." *Nuestras Comidas* 55-60. San José: Coordinación Educativa y Cultural Centroamericana (CECC), Serie Culturas Populares Centroamericanas, No. 4, 2001.

Oviero, Ramón, and Maritza Rivera. "Panamá: Comidas regionales." *Nuestras Comidas* 223-228.

---. "Panamá: Bebidas populares." *Nuestras Comidas* 267-269.

Oviero, Ramón, and Pedro Prado. "Panamá: Alimentos de otros orígenes." *Nuestras Comidas* 117-120.

"Panama Canal Museum Holiday Collectible Ornaments-2006: The Tivoli Hotel, 1906-1971. *Panamacanalmuseum. org.* Panama Canal Museum, n.d. Web. 2 Apr. 2012.

"Panama Canal Review." *Latin American Collection: University of Florida Digital Collections* (2010): n. pag. Web. 4 Apr. 2012.

"Panama: First-World Convenience at Third-World Prices." *International Living.com.* International Living Mag., n.d. Web. 30 Mar. 2012.

Peláez, Berta de. *Cocina Panameña.* Distribuidora Lewis, Panamá, 1997.

Pérez, Amelia de, Angeli Gandhi, and Rosita Shahani. "Evolución histórico-demográfica de la comunidad hindostana de Panamá (1976)." *Panamá en sus usos y costumbres.* Ed.

Stanley Heckadon Moreno. Tomo 14, Panamá: Editorial Universitaria, 1994. 107-135.

"Personajes Afro-panameños destacados: Bayano, Antón Mandinga, Luis de Mozambique." *Afrohispanos.org.* Afro Hispanos Mag., n.d. Web. 8 Feb. 2011.

Ponce, Tamara. "Mono en Bijao Festival." *Folklore. PanamaTipico.com,* 31 July 2010. Web. 25 Apr. 2012.

"Recipes from Panama." *Panamaliving.com.* Panama Living, 28 Jan. 2006. Web. 1 Jun. 2011.

ReyPrensa. *Recetario. Prensa.com,* n.d. Web. 23 Jan 2012.

ReyPrensa. *Recetario. Prensa.com,* n.d. Web. 24 Jan 2012.

Rogers, Muriel. Letters and Notes (with recipes) to the authors. 20 March 2012.

Rogers, Rosa. Personal Interview. 17 November 2010.

SomosPanama.com. Somos Panamá, n.d. Web. 14 Jun. 2011

Tyler Herbst, Sharon, and Ron Herbst. *The New Food Lover's Companion.* 4th ed. Barron's Educational Series, 2007.

Torres de Araúz, Reina. "Panorama actual de las culturas indígenas panameñas (1972)." *Panamá en sus usos y costumbres.* Ed. Stanley Heckadon Moreno. Tomo 14, Panamá: Editorial Universitaria, 1994. 23-43.

Tu Mañana- Recetas. "Empanada de Maíz con Pollo." *Telemetro.com.* Canal 13 Panama-Telemetro.com, 6 Nov. 2008. Web. 27 Oct. 2011.

Valdés, Grethel. "Receta No 10. "Rosca de Huevo/Recipe No.10 Egg Bread." *cocinava.blospot.com.* Cocinova, 26 Nov. 2006. Web. 23 Jun. 2011.

"Wheat." *Botanical-online.com.* Botanical, n.d. Web. 12 Jun. 2012.

XLVI Feria Internacional de San José de David. *Recetario Panameño.* Panamá, March, 2001.

Yolitas "Re: Día de la Etnia Negra en Panamá." *Yolitas Decoraciones.* Yolitas.Blogspot, n.d. Web. 7 Dec. 2011.

Zoveida Ruiz, Olga. Personal Interview. 14 November 2010.

GLOSSARY

Ackee (Ackee or Akí): Native to tropical West Africa. The ackee or vegetable brain is a bright red tropical fruit with black seeds. When ripe, it has a soft and creamy white flesh.

Ají chombo: A variety of the *Capsicum Chinense* from Chinese origin. It is heavily grown and used in the Caribbean and Central America. Ají chombo is a type of Scotch Bonnet used in Panama; it is a very hot chili pepper. The name ají chombo literally means black man's hot pepper, deriving from the word "chombo" used to refer to an Afro-Panamanian man. They range in color from light green, yellow, and red. Ají chombo is mainly used to make hot sauces. They are also used in its original form to spice up some dishes.

Allspice (Pimienta de Jamaica): Native to the West Indies, especially Jamaica; Mexico, Honduras, Guatemala, and Cuba. Allspice is a berry that is dried and ground to make an aromatic powder. Its flavor is a combination of cinnamon, clove, and nutmeg. Allspice is used in cakes and other pastries. It is also used in spice mixes and in curries.

Annatto (Achiote): Native to South America. It has spread in popularity to Central America, Mexico, Africa, and Asia. It is derived from the seeds of the achiote trees of tropical and subtropical areas around the world. When mature, this heart-shaped fruit is brown or reddish brown and it is covered with short, stiff hairs. At maturity it splits open and exposes the dark red seeds. The annatto food coloring (orange to red) is prepared by simmering the seeds in water or oil. In Latin America is better known as achiote and it is commonly used to color and flavor foods. Across Latin America, many natives also use it to paint their bodies and lips.

Avocado (Aguacate): It was first named *ahuácatl* by the Aztecs in Mexico. The avocado is native to the Americas. There are several varieties, but all of them have an oval shape and their skin color ranges from green to purple. The flesh has a buttery texture when ripe.

Banana (Guineo): Bananas are believed to be originated in Malaysia, spreading to India and the Philippines. Bananas have a sweet creamy firm flesh with a skin that is deep green when not ripe and yellow when ripe. In Panama, it is known as guineo and banana/o.

Barley (Cebada): It is believed to have originated in southeast Asia and Ethiopia. Subsequently, it spread to Europe, North America, and to the rest of the world. Barley resembles wheat berries, but they are lighter in color. The barley sprouts are used to make malt syrup that when fermented is base for beer and other alcoholic beverages.

Basil (Albahaca): It was called the "royal herb" by ancient Greeks. This annual plant is a member of the mint family. Fresh basil has a pungent flavor that some describe as a cross between licorice and cloves. Most varieties of basil have green leaves, such as lemon and cinnamon basil. Others like opal basil are purple. Their perfumed fragrance and flavors match their respective names.

Breadfruit (Arbol de pan): Native to the Pacific, breadfruit is large (8 to 10 inches in diameter), and it has a bumpy green skin and a rather bland-tasting cream-colored center. It is picked and eaten before it ripens and before it becomes too sweet (Tyler Herbst).

Callaloo or kallaloo (Kalalú or Calalú): It is also known as water spinach in the Caribbean. Kallaloo is a leaf vegetable and it is also the name of a popular Caribbean dish.

Cane Syrup (Miel de caña): It is produced by evaporating the juice from sugar cane to make a thick, amber-colored syrup. Cane syrup is incorrectly known as unsulphured molasses.

Cashew Apple (Marañón): Native to the northeast of Brazil. The cashew fruit is referred as a pseudo fruit. In the United States, the cashew nut is more desirable than the cashew apple. In Brazil, Panama, and the Caribbean cashew apple is regarded as a delicacy.

Chayote Squash (Chayote - Some Afro-Panamanians call it Chocho): It is believed that chayote was cultivated in Mexico since pre-Columbus times. It is widely used and grown in Central America and the Caribbean. It is a relative of the cucumber and the squash. The fruit is bland -tasting and it's used in soups, purees, and stews.

Chile Peppers (Chiles): They belong to the family of the *Capsicum* and they include a wide variety of hot peppers that differ in shape, color, size, and hotness.

Chiltepe/Bird's Eye (Chiltepe chile): Native to the Americas. The Chiltepin Chili is a small chili that is very hot without the chili pepper taste.

Chipotle: The Aztecs named it *chilpoctli*, a *nahuatl* word that literally means "smoked chili pepper." It is really a smoke-dried jalapeño pepper, commonly used in the Mexican cuisine. Chipotle has become very popular in the United States.

Cinnamon (Canela): It is one of the oldest spices and can be traced before biblical times. There are two well-known varieties: the Ceylon and the Chinese cinnamon (cassia). Cinnamon comes from the bark of the cinnamon tree which is dried in the shape of sticks. It can easily be made into powder.

The Ceylon cinnamon is considered of a sweeter and higher quality.

Cloves (Clavito de Olor): Native to the Moluccas Islands in Indonesia. Cloves are grown commercially in Eastern Africa, The West Indies, Tropical Asia, and Brazil. They are the unopened flower buds of an evergreen clove tree, which are dried until they turn black in color. Cloves are usually used sparingly to add flavor to sweet and savory dishes.

Cocoa (Cacao): Native to the Americas. Cocoa is the fruit from the cacao tree (*Theobroma Cacao*). It is cultivated in Mexico, Central and South America, Africa, some Caribbean islands, and some South Pacific islands.

Coconut (Coco): Kenneth Olsen, a plant evolutionary biologist, and his colleagues collected and examined coconut DNA. This study suggests that there are two origins of cultivation of the coconut: the Pacific basin (southeast Asia) and the Indian basin (southern periphery of India, including Sri Lanka, the Maldives, and the Laccadives). The two origins of cultivation are different genetically. Indian type coconut was brought to the New World by Europeans. "The Portuguese carried coconuts from the Indian Ocean to the West Coast of Africa. According to Olsen, the plantations established there were a source of material that made it into the Caribbean and also to coastal Brazil." Spanish carried Pacific type coconuts to the Pacific coast of Mexico. Consequently, one can find both types in the Americas. Pacific type coconuts can be found on the Pacific coast of Central America and Indian type coconuts on the Atlantic coast. In addition, the study reveals that "coconut genetics also preserve a record of prehistoric trade routes and of the colonization of the Americas…Traditionally, coconuts have been classified into tall and dwarf varieties based on the tree 'habit,' or shape… Most coconuts are tall" (Science Daily).

Coffee (Café): Ethiopia is thought to be the motherland of the first coffee beans which, throughout the ages, found their way to Brazil and Colombia — the two largest coffee producers today. Coffee plantations abound throughout other South and Central American countries, Cuba, Hawaii, Indonesia, Jamaica, and many African nations. There are hundreds of different coffee species but the two most commercially viable are *coffea robusta* and *coffea arabica*.

Cilantro: (also called *Chinese parsley* and *coriander*) has bright green leaves and stems, a lively, strong fragrance that some describe as "soapy." It is widely used in the Asian, Caribbean, and Latin American cuisines.

Coriander: Native to the Mediterranean and the Orient. It's the seed of the cilantro plant. Mention of coriander seeds was found in early Sanskrit writings and the seeds themselves have been discovered in Egyptian tombs dating back to 960 B.C. Coriander is used widely in the Indian, Mexican, Asian, and Caribbean cuisines.

Corozo: Native to Costa Rica, Panama, Colombia, Venezuela, and the Atlantic Area of South America. The corozo palm bears a dark red fruit that grows in clusters. It is used to make drinks, jams, and wines. The seed and skin are used to feed pigs. The oil from the seeds is used to make hair grease, oils, soaps, and other products. The seeds are used to fabricate buttons.

Culantro de coyote: Native to Latin America and the Caribbean. It is widely used in Thailand, Malaysia, and Singapore. Culantro is associated with cilantro but they are not the same. It has elongated serrated leaves and a strong distinct aroma. Culantro is a key ingredient in Panamanian cuisine.

Currants (Pasa de Corinto): Currants can be traced back to Ancient Greece. Currants are small dried raisins from the Black Corinth grapes. The major producers are California, South Africa, and Australia. Currants are mostly used in baked goods.

Date (Dátil): Native to North Africa and West Asia. Fruit from a palm tree or *Palma Real (Phoenix dactylifera)*.

European Onions (Cebollas europeas): A number of onions are native to Europe: red onion and a spring/salad onion from Italy and a sweet onion from the southeast of France.

Garlic (Ajo or ajillo): Central Asia is considered its place of origin. Some of its close relatives are onion, shallot, leek, and chives. When cooked, garlic becomes sweet and milder in flavor, giving dishes a good taste, especially sauces, meats, and poultry.

Ginger (Jengibre): *Zingiber officinale* can be traced to tropical Asia where it was used both for medicinal and culinary purpose.

Green Onions (Cebollina): It has been consumed since pre-historic times. They are from the same family of the onions and leeks, they are also called scallions. Green onions are young onions that are harvested before they develop into a full onion; and scallions are younger than green onions, they are picked before the bulb starts to develop. Both, green onions and scallions are green cylindrical green shoots that are used in recipes. The green and white parts of scallions are used equally, but the green part of the green onion is used separately from the white.

Guava (Guayaba): Indigenous to Central America and Mexico. It grows in almost every tropical country. Guava is round or oval. The skin ranges from green to maroon and the flesh can be white to deep pink; it is usually sweet, but some can be sour.

Habanero Pepper (Habanero): It is believed to be of Cuban origin and then it spread in popularity from Mexico to the rest of Central America. Habanero pepper is one of the hottest peppers on the heat scale. They vary in color from green, red, orange, and even white; they have a citrus like fruity flavor, and they are round or oblong. Habaneros are confused with the Scotch Bonnet, but the habaneros have a slightly different flavor and they are shaped differently.

Harts of Palms (Palmito): It is harvested from the inner core and growing buds of palm trees. The most popular varieties come from the peach palm and the cabbage palm. The main cultivators of this vegetable are Costa Rica and part of South America.

Jobo (Mombin or Hog Plum): Native to Mexico, Central America, parts of South America, and the West Indies. Another variety is purple mombin which is the most desirable of the two. The yellow mombin grows in clusters of a dozen or more, it is a small yellow and oval fruit. Its juice is a bit acid.

Kidney Beans (Frijoles): They derived from a common bean ancestor that originated in Peru, spreading out throughout South and Central America. Today, the major producers of kidney beans are India, China, Indonesia, and the United States.

Lemon (Limón amarillo): The origin is not clear, but it's believed that the origin of cultivation is India and China. There is an extensive variety of lemons that are produced through experimentation of the major growers like Florida. Lemons are oval usually with a yellow textured peel and a pale yellow flesh incased in 8 to 10 segments. Lemons have a tart, acidic taste, but they add a great flavor to foods and drinks.

Lemongrass or Herbal Lemon (Limoncillo): It's of Malaysian origin and it's cultivated in tropical and subtropical areas. The species mostly used in Panama is the *Cymbopogon citratrus* (grown in the West Indies). Lemongrass is a perennial grass family of the sugar cane, with a lemon taste. It is used in herbal teas, beverages and other dishes. In Panama is also known as *Marucha*. Afro-Panamanians also call it fever grass.

Lentils (Lentejas): Its origin of cultivation appears to be Central Asia and the Near East. Lentils are a legume that includes a large variety of colors (brown, green, black, yellow, and orange) and types.

Lima or Sweet Lime (Lima dulce): Native to India. Sweet lime is also grown in Egypt, the Near East, and Latin America. In the United States, sweet lime is grown in very limited areas, due to the inconsistency of its flavor and size. They can be found mostly for sale in Latin markets. Sweet limes are the size and shape of an orange and the skin is lemon yellow. They have a mild-sweet, acid taste.

Lime (Limón): It is believed that its origin of cultivation is the Indo-Malayan region. Limes are smaller than lemons, and they range in color from green to yellowish green. Limes are usually more sour than lemon. They are preferred when preparing alcoholic drinks. Lemons and limes are both used with sugar to make aides and also to flavor foods.

Mace and Nutmeg (Macis y Nuez Moscada): Native to the

Banda Islands (Indonesia). Mace and nutmeg come from the same tree; mace is the outer cover of the seed (nutmeg). The mace is dried in the sun and then separated from the nutmeg and either used whole or ground in dishes that require a more delicate spice. Nutmeg has a more pungent taste and is mostly used in sweet dishes. Mace can be used in seafood dishes.

Malanga (Otoe and Ñampí):   Native to Southeast Asia. The variety native to East and West Africa was spread to the Caribbean and the Americas. Malanga is a perennial plant as long as is not harvested. The cormels are underground plant stems of a plant similar to bulbs. Some are used for consumption. The otoe has a brown-rough bark with small growths, and white or yellow flesh (flesh turns light purple when cooked). Ñampí is another variety of malanga. Ñampí (or chamol) is of the *eddoe* type which is smaller than the malanga or dasheen.

Mamey Sapote: Sapote/zapote (Mamey) comes from the *nahual* word *tzapotl*. The fruit is native to Mexico, Central America, the Caribbean, and tropical South America. In Panama it's known as *Mamey*. Sapote or Mamey is usually oval to round and pointy at the apex. Its skin is brown and thick, and its flesh color ranges from salmon pink to dark red. It has a sweet pumpkin-like taste.

Marjoram   (Mejorana/Amaraco):   Native   to   the Mediterranean, North Africa, and Asia. The Marjoram plant has small deep green oval leaves that are used either dried or fresh. They are used to flavor fish, salads, sausages, vegetables, pork, and meats.

Melon (Melón): Native to Central Africa. It is a name given to various members of the plant family with fleshy fruit (gourds or cucurbits). Melon can be referred as a plant or a fruit. Although the melon is a fruit, some varieties may be considered "culinary vegetables."

Molasses (Miel de caña): It was the preferred sweetener in the United States because it was less expensive than refined sugar. All this changed after World War I when the price of sugar dropped. Now, molasses is more expensive than refined sugar. Molasses is a by-product of sugar cane, resulting from the process of extracting sugar from sugar cane or sugar beets. In this process the juice of the sugar cane or sugar beets is boiled until the sugar is crystalized and the leftover syrup is called molasses. There are two varieties of molasses: light molasses (extracted from the first boiling) and dark molasses (the product of the second boiling). Light molasses is sweeter than dark molasses.

Nance: Native to Southern Mexico, the Pacific Central America, Peru, Brazil, and parts of the Caribbean. The fruit is cherry-like in shape, with a yellow-orange skin. Nance has a distinctive odor, and when made into drinks it gives the beverage an oily film. This small tropical fruit has culinary and beverage uses across Central America and northern South America_ It has different names, and it's sometimes called "wild cherry" in Panama.

Naranjilla: It is believed to be native to Peru, Ecuador, and Columbia. The naranjilla grown in Panama was a result of a planting effort of graphed plants by commercial fruit growers in the 1950s. This variety is larger than the original fruit. The naranjilla fruit is round and when ripe it shows a bright yellow skin with green-yellowish translucent pulp with small seeds. The pulp has a citrusy flavor. It's mostly used for its juice.

Ñame: This tuber is popular in South and Central America, the West Indies and parts of Asia and Africa. Ñame is a long, round tuber with brown skin and off-white flesh. It should not be confused with yam.

Olive (Aceituna): Native to the Mediterranean area, the olive is a small, oily fruit that contains a pit. It's grown for its fruit and its oil in subtropical zones. Olive varieties number in the dozens and vary in size and flavor.

Oregano (Orégano): Native to the Mediterranean. It is closely related to marjoram, but oregano is a larger plant with rounder leaves and a much stronger flavor than marjoram. Oregano has a strong peppery taste, and it is used mainly to flavor beef, lamb, and pork.

Palm oil; palm-kernel oil (Aceite de palma): The reddish-orange oil extracted from the pulp of the fruit of the African palm. The fruit grows throughout tropical Africa.

Parsley (Perejíl): It is difficult to identify the origin of parsley, but it is believed that parley has its origin in the Mediterranean region. There are a few varieties of parsley, but the most common is the curled parsley. This parsley has a mild and distinctive flavor. The other variety is the Italian or flat leaf parsley, it has a stronger flavor that the curled parsley, but it is less bitter. Another variety of parsley is the Hamburg or turnip-rooted. This parsley is cultivated more for its bulb -like roots that are eaten as a vegetable. Parsley is mostly used as garnish, in soups, sauces, garlic bread and other dishes. Parsley is rich in antioxidants and it is usually known to suppress the smell of strong foods like garlic.

Passion Fruit, Granadilla (Purple and Yellow Variety): *Passiflora edulis / P. edulis flavicarpa* is native to South America (from southern Brazil through Paraguay to northern Argentina). This egg-shaped tropical fruit has a highly aromatic, jelly-like orange pulp. Its seeds are edible. Passion fruit is commonly used as a flavoring for beverages and sauces. Major growers in the world are Brazil, Hawaii, Florida, California, and New Zealand. Passion fruit drink is very popular in Panama. Passion fruit names: mburucuyá (Argentina, Paraguay, Uruguay), maracujá (Brazil and Portugal), maracuyá-yelow variety and gulupa – purple variety (Colombia), maracuyá (Bolivia, Costa Rica, Panama, Ecuador, Mexico, Honduras, Peru), chinola (Dominican Republic), calala (Nicaragua), parcha (Puerto Rico), parchita (Venzuela), granadilla (South Africa), sweet cup (Jamaica), lilikoi (Hawaii), markisa (Indonesia).

Peach Palm Fruit (Pejibaye or Pixbae): Native to the Amazons (Ecuador, Colombia, Brazil, and Peru) and it is abundant in Costa Rica, Nicaragua, Honduras, and Panama where it's grown commercially to be sold in local markets or by street vendors. Pejibaye is grown in clusters of about 50 to 100 that hang from the peach palm. It has a small round to oval shape and the skin can range from yellow-green to orange-red. Pejibaye has to be boiled before consumption; it also has a seed in most varieties that can be eaten by cracking the outer shell.

Peppermint (Hierba Buena/Yerba Buena): There are many varieties of mint that differ from region to region. Mint is used either fresh or dried in drinks, salads, meats (mostly lamb). This herb has a lemon odor when crushed. *Mentha citrata* has many medicinal and aromatic properties.

Pumpkin (Ahuyama): *Ayote* o *ayotl* in the Aztec language *nahuatl*. It is believed to be of Asian origin, but it is known to be domesticated and cultivated in Latin America. In Panama, pumpkin or winter squash is known as ahuyama and zapallo. It varies in shape from oval to globe-like and its flesh is orange or yellow-green. It can be mildly sweet to very sweet.

Quince (Membrillo): Native to the mountainous region of northern Turkey, Iran, and southern Georgia. The quince is part of the pear and apple family; it is pear-shaped and bright yellow. It is hard, fragrant, and sour. Quince is used cooked to make jams and jellies. It can also be combined with apples in pastries.

Soursop (Guanábana): It grows throughout the West Indies, in southern Mexico and parts of South America. The soursop fruit is oval in shape. When ripe, it has yellow-green skin and it has soft protruding spines. The flesh is cream in color with black seed and a pungent acid-sweet flavor.

Sugar Cane (Caña de azúcar): Native to tropical regions of Asia. This grass-like plant has stout, jointed, fibrous stalks that are rich in sugar. Sugar cane is indigenous to tropical south Asia and southeast Asia. Spaniards introduced it to the Caribbean and later on the plant made it to America. The juice from the sugar cane is processed and used in foods for humans and animals. The fermented juice is used to make alcoholic beverages.

Sweet Potato (Camote): Native to tropical South America. There are several varieties, the orange and the white sweet potato. The orange is commonly used in the southern region of the United States; the white sweet potato is mostly used in the rest of the Americas and the Caribbean.

Tamarind (Tamarindo): Native to tropical Africa. The tree produces the tamarind fruit. The fruit has a fleshy, juicy, acidulous pulp. It is mature when the flesh is brown or reddish-brown.

Thyme (Tomillo): It dates back to ancient Egypt and Greece for medicinal purposes. It is native to Asia. There are about sixty varieties of thyme, some of them are common thyme (comes in three varieties: brad-leaved, narrow, narrow-leaved, variegated-leaved), lemon thyme, orange thyme, and silver thyme. Thyme is an aromatic herb with small gray-green leaves. It can be used either dried or fresh.

Vanilla (Vainilla): It is indigenous to southeast Mexico and parts of Central America. Vanilla is an essence used to flavor desserts or sweet dishes.

Watercress (Berro): It is thought to have originated in Europe. Watercress has small, crisp, dark green leaves. Its pungent flavor is slightly bitter and has a peppery snap.

Watermelon (Sandía): It is native to Africa. Watermelon is the fruit of a vine-like plant and is one of the most common types of melon. The watermelon is juicy and sweet. When ripe its flesh is usually pink, but sometimes orange, yellow or red.

Wheat (Trigo): It is believed that the cultivation of wheat started about 10,000 to 12,000 years ago from wild species harvested by ancient hunter-gatherers in southeast Asia. Subsequently, it spread to other parts of the world and it was widely cultivated in the Turkestan region, southern Europe, Egypt, and Rome. It was brought to the Americas by Spanish and English. Today, wheat is cultivated in most parts of the world and there are many varieties. Most of the wheat production is used for wheat flour. The major producing countries are China, the United States, Russia, Ukraine, and France.

Yuca/Cassava (Yuca): Native to western and southern Mexico and parts of Guatemala and Brazil. It is a starchy woody root used in the preparation of cassava flour and tapioca. This root vegetable is also used much like a potato. Its name is spelled "yuca or yucca." A noteworthy fact is that the word "yucca" refers to a genus of perennial shrubs or trees of the family *asparagaceae*.

INDEX

DESSERTS AND SWEETS

Alfajor, 390
Bienmesabe, 393
Bocado de la Reina, 386
Bocado del Rey, 388
Buñuelos de Pascua, 423
Cabanga, 398
Candied Pumpkin Squash, 378
Cashew Fruit Marmalade, 397
Claritas, 418
Cocada, 395
Cocada with Cashews, 396
Cofio, 411
Corn Pudding, 414
Darien's Angel Hair, 413
Enyucado, 375
Fruit Cake, 425
Huevitos de Leche, 401
Guisadas, 421
Mamallena, 370
Mango Mousse, 404
Manjar Blanco, 392
Mary Jane Cookies, 376
Mazamorra, 366
Meringues, 402
Orange Flan, 416
Panamanian Taffy, 399
Peach Palm Fruit Flan, 371
Queques, 369
Red Bean Pie, 379
Rice Chocolate Pudding and Coconut Milk, 410
Rice Pudding, 406
Rice Pudding Chiriqui-Style, 408
Rice with Raisins, 412
Rosquitos, 419
Sopa Borracha, 381
Sopa de Gloria, 384
Sour Orange Candy, 417
Suripico, 368

PASTA AND NOODLES

PLANTAINS AND BANANAS

PORK, BEEF, AND OTHER MEATS

POULTRY

RICE

Would you like to see your manuscript become a book?

If you are interested in becoming a PublishAmerica author, please submit your manuscript for possible publication to us at:

acquisitions@publishamerica.com

You may also mail in your manuscript to:

**PublishAmerica
PO Box 151
Frederick, MD 21705**

We also offer free graphics for Children's Picture Books!

---

www.publishamerica.com

CPSIA information can be obtained
at www.ICGtesting.com
Printed in the USA
BVOW08*0558291216
472047BV00003B/12/P